The 52-Week Low
Formula

The 52-Week Low Formula

A CONTRARIAN STRATEGY THAT LOWERS RISK, BEATS THE MARKET, AND OVERCOMES HUMAN EMOTION

Luke L. Wiley, CFP®

WILEY

Published by John Wiley & Sons, Inc., Hoboken, New Jersey.
Published simultaneously in Canada.

For general information on our other products and services or for technical support, please contact our Customer Care Department within the United States at (800) 762-2974, outside the United States at (317) 572-3993, or fax (317) 572-4002.

Wiley publishes in a variety of print and electronic formats and by print-on-demand. Some material included with standard print versions of this book may not be included in e-books or in print-on-demand. If this book refers to media such as a CD or DVD that is not included in the version you purchased, you may download this material at http://booksupport.wiley.com. For more information about Wiley products, visit www.wiley.com.

Library of Congress Cataloging-in-Publication Data:
Wiley, Luke L., 1975–
    The 52-week low formula : a contrarian strategy that lowers risk, beats the market, and overcomes human emotion/Luke L. Wiley.
        pages cm
    Includes index.
        ISBN 978-1-118-85347-4 (cloth); ISBN 978-1-118-85353-5 (ePDF);
ISBN 978-1-118-85357-3 (ePub)
        1. Investments.   2. Success in business.   3. Competition.   I. Title.
II. Title: Fifty-two week low formula.
    HG4521.W4764 2014
    332.6–dc23
                                                                2013051133

Printed in the United States of America.
10 9 8 7 6 5 4 3 2 1

To the five most candid and loving board of advisors who help me become the person they know I am capable of becoming:

my wife, Melissa (Grounded)
daughter, Madyson (Justice)
son, Jake (Humility)
daughter, Leah (Strength)
daughter, Morgan (Joy)

There is one side to the stock market; and it is not the bull side or bear side, but the right side.

—Reminiscences of a Stock Operator
by Edwin LeFevre, 1923

The conventional view serves to protect us from the painful job of thinking.

—John Kenneth Galbraith

There is nothing like losing all you have in the world for teaching you what not to do. And when you know what not to do in order to lose money, you begin to learn what to do in order to win. Did you get that? You begin to learn!

—Reminiscences of a Stock Operator
by Edwin LeFevre, 1923

The only function of economic forecasting is to make astrology look respectable.

—John Kenneth Galbraith

The simpleton believes everything, but the shrewd man measures his steps.

—Proverbs 14:15

The 52-Week Low Five Filter Formula

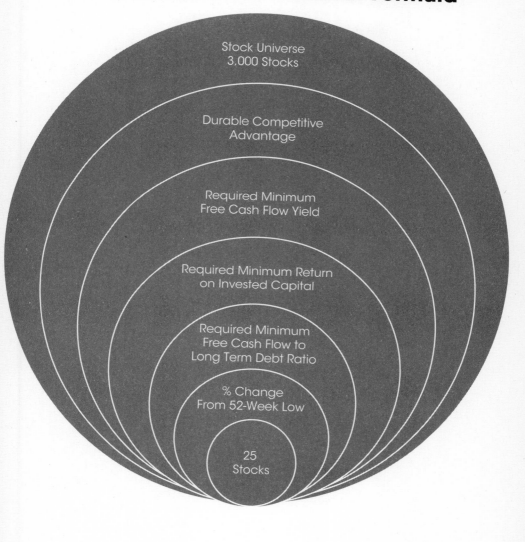

Stock Universe
3,000 Stocks

Durable Competitive
Advantage

Required Minimum
Free Cash Flow Yield

Required Minimum Return
on Invested Capital

Required Minimum
Free Cash Flow to
Long Term Debt Ratio

% Change
From 52-Week Low

25
Stocks

Contents

Introduction

Would you like to become a mediocre investor? Do you have an interest in buying high and selling low? Do you seek out information that only confirms your beliefs and emotions? Do you believe the stock market is merely a crapshoot and only the ultra-wealthy make money in it?

If you are answering "no" to all or most of the preceding questions or would like to answer no to them, then I believe my book will help you achieve the opposite of those questions—instead of mediocrity, you can achieve far better. My strategy, if properly followed, can insulate you from mediocre investment results. This book explains how to more effectively buy low and sell high on an ongoing basis. It is also a book about how to be a better thinker in many areas of your life.

I am the last person I ever thought would write a book. In fact, in my senior year of high school I took calculus twice, not because I failed the first semester but because I actually had a knack for math, and it was the highest level of math offered. I actually thought I would be a math teacher. In fact, it is sad to say that I read only one book in high school, and that was reflected in my substandard scores on the high school aptitude tests due to my below-average English skills. I was the guy who scored substandard on my ACTs, the guy sweating up a storm on the soccer field, the kid who shopped at the Salvation Army while my classmates went to the Gap. In my young life, it would have been hard to imagine reading a book, let alone having enough to say to write one.

Then again, maybe it wasn't so surprising because I've never been one to conform to conventional wisdom and, despite my standardized test scores, I have had one big advantage over a lot of other people: a willingness to learn and an internal fire to disprove some of the widely held beliefs of society that kept me working long after most other people would have given up.

I grew up in a military family. My dad was in the Air Force and we moved around quite a lot when I was young, eventually settling in Florida. I was the oldest of the three brothers, the one who went first in everything. In those important developmental years, I was always the new kid in class. To many, this would have been a disadvantage, but without the influence of an older sibling and constantly having to make new friends, I was given a gift—a blank slate on which to form my own opinions and approaches. I think it was a blessing that my parents had me at age 18 and that we shopped at the Salvation Army until I was 12, when my father received his bachelor's degree in mechanical engineering. My parents showed me through their actions the value of doing things that go against the status quo—young parents, young marriage, college degree midway through career, the value of a dollar, delayed gratification, and many other actions that challenged the norm.

It would be years before I would read a book by Berkshire Hathaway cofounder Charlie Munger and learn about the seventeenth-century German mathematician Carl Gustav Jacob Jacobi and his cardinal rule: "invert, always invert." That cardinal rule would become my mantra, the way I thought, the way I solved problems in later years, but I think I innately understood what Jacobi was talking about early on in my life, that many of the hardest problems in life are best solved in reverse. It had been the way I lived my life.

Inversion, the way Jacobi described it, is the process of solving problems by first understanding the opposite approach.

Understand a desired outcome and, rather than designing a solution for that outcome, design the solution for the opposite. If you are trying to be healthy, figure out all the steps and processes that would make you sick and do the opposite. If you want to build wealth and be financially successful, figure out all the steps that will ensure that you will become destitute and do the opposite. To hit this critical thinking exercise home, I would like to share with you some of the key points within the commencement speech given by Charlie Munger in 1986 to the Harvard School.

Charlie did not tell the graduating class all the ways to be successful but actually laid out the prescriptions for guaranteed misery in life. He expanded on Johnny Carson's three prescriptions to guarantee misery:

1. Be unreliable.
2. Learn only from your own personal experience; minimize what you learn from others.
3. Go down and stay down when you get your first, second, and third severe reverses in the battle of life.

I have actually applied this inversion to my marriage. Instead of asking yourself how you can have a fulfilling marriage, ask yourself: What are the surest ways to have a miserable marriage? Or the extreme—what are the surest ways to destroy my marriage? Or get a lack of respect from my kids? Or live a life of mediocrity? In fact, when I think about it, I pretty much think this way consistently. It is not that I am a pessimist; quite the opposite, actually. I try to think about the negative consequences first, and then strive to make the right choices. Do you remember when you were a kid and you set out to complete the hardest mazes? When you started at the end of the maze, you were more likely to be successful at completing it, and faster than others who took the common path—starting at the beginning.

If you want to build wealth above and beyond the average, figure out how to attain the average and work backwards from there. If you are the new kid in a school and want to make a bunch of new friends, figure out how you would fail and avoid those steps.

It works like this.

Identify the desired outcome:

I want to be a successful investor throughout my lifetime.

Inverse:

I want to find the proven ways to be unsuccessful as an investor.

Solve for the inverse:

What are the behaviors, the messages from the investment world, the mindset, the emotions, and the investment strategy that could help me guarantee substandard and quite disappointing investment results?

Do the opposite:

Seek out research that refutes your deeply held beliefs about investing. Seek out individuals, both living and dead, who you can learn from to help insulate you from poor decision making. Take time to objectively study the lack of accuracy of economic forecasts and analysts' recommendations. Make it a point to understand the various human biases that can negatively impact your desired outcome. Develop a strategy that is built on logic and value and not on emotion and enthusiasm.

This is, in essence, the exact exercise I performed several years ago. I was determined to find a better way forward for our clients, my family, my parents, and future grandchildren.

Had I been like thousands of other high school seniors who achieved less-than-spectacular results on standardized exams, I might have followed a path of less resistance. I would have gone to school and skated by. But a substandard aptitude test in high school was the spark I needed to take a hard look at how to disprove what these tests were forecasting about my future potential. The aptitude tests revealed the potential outcome of my life and helped me realize that what lay ahead was the opposite of the outcome I desired. What followed was a Division I soccer scholarship and a collegiate career built on dean's list performance while carrying three very challenging majors: finance, economics, and real estate. I forced myself to outwork and outthink all my peers because I knew what I didn't want. I knew I didn't want to be just another average student with just another average postcollege career. I wanted more and rose to the challenge.

All this may seem like I am bragging. It may seem like I'm giving you a resume, and I suppose, in a way, I am. But not for the reason you might assume. I mention some of my experiences to help you understand the journey I made on the way to writing this book. I mention overperforming in college to help explain the way I think, because all of these experiences and attributes were at play when I began my career in finance. And they are certainly not unique to me. Think of the most successful people you know. I'd be willing to bet very few of them have settled for their lot in life. Successful people are generally successful thinkers. They begin with the end, and rather than simply laying a sequential plan for getting there, they think of the things that will get in the way and make their plans to compensate for those challenges. They identify the potential problems and avoid them, and they do so with vigor. Some do it consciously, some do it instinctively, but I'd be willing to invest in the notion that they all do it— they solve for the inverse.

Henry David Thoreau once said, "Most men lead lives of quiet desperation and go to the grave with a song still in them." He was talking about living an action-oriented life, but you can take that same idea and realize that what he was also talking about was hope. Hope is a troubling emotion. Economists would probably link hope to the sunk-cost cognitive bias. You've invested in your life, your education, your career, and your portfolio, with the hope that it will result in something fulfilling, something rich, something to quench your quiet desperation. What is actually happening is that you are following a path without a clear destination in mind.

If fitting in in junior high is about conformity, the world of finance is the largest seventh-grade lunchroom in the world. True, there are plenty of examples of the exceptions. You will read many references to Warren Buffett in the pages that follow. But for every Buffett or Munger, there are literally thousands of men and women selling the same mutual funds recommended by the same analysts, and packaged by the same companies.

Why? Well, for one thing, it's easy. A college graduate can make a nice living recommending index funds and mutual funds. There's safety in it. The old adage "no one ever got fired for buying IBM" was meant to describe the complacency of technology purchasing a couple of decades ago, but it is perhaps even truer in the investing world. No one ever got fired for buying the Standard & Poor's (S&P) 500 Index or the most admired mutual fund. So the safety makes it easy. But, more than that, there seems to be a lack of healthy skepticism in many of the financial professionals I have come across over the years.

In addition to the quote from Jacobi, one of my favorite quotes is from President Ronald Reagan, who said when describing U.S./USSR relations, "Trust, but verify." It means that it's okay to trust the way things are done, so long as you have the stamina and dedication to understand why they are done. I'm a trusting person, but I'm also the kind of person who does his homework. College and the sense that I needed to change the path that I had created for myself with substandard test scores proved the value in double-checking conventional wisdom. Take the time and make the effort to understand before blindly following the path in front of you. The result will help you understand the logic behind choices that are commonly made, and also to begin to comprehend their shortcomings.

This is what happened to me as a young financial professional. I toed the party line. I sold the securities recommended by the analysts and even allowed myself to get caught up in the headlines, hype, and talking heads on cable television. I tried to keep up when I should have been digging in and asking questions. Eventually, I began to ask questions. I trusted the analysts and the products, but I began the process of verifying them, and what I found was a better way.

I've spent over 15 years perfecting that better way, molding and shaping it. I've worked with clients and sought experts. I've paid for my own research and invested my own money. I've taken losses and made gains, all in the name of verification. I've inverted nearly every aspect of investing—not just the mechanical and financial side of it, but the emotional and social forces that influence the way we make investing decisions. And the result of this relentless pursuit is the book you are holding now and the principles behind the 52-Week Low formula.

There are literally thousands of investing books. Many of them make big promises about overnight gains. Many of them make claims of extraordinary gains in unprecedented short periods of time. A lot of them want to tell you the "secrets" of investing. I've read a lot of them. I've dissected them. And I have concluded:

- There are no "secrets" to investing well. Good investing comes from strategy and process, not from uncovering some never-before-seen corner of the market. The only rule that really applies is this: buy low, sell high. On the surface, it is simple and it should be.
- Too many of us overcomplicate investing. We don't do it knowingly. It just happens. We get caught up in the hype. We have an instinct to follow the herd. We allow

emotions—namely, hope and fear—to cloud our judgments. Investing is not as simple as, say, chewing gum, but it doesn't need to be as complicated as we often make it out to be. We get in our own way when we don't have a process that mandates simplicity.

- There is no magic wand. Just because you heard a tip from a guy who knows a guy who knows Bill Gates does not mean you know anything at all. Trying to bet on the next big thing is not investing; it is gambling. Feel free to do it, but don't play with your mortgage money. I often tell clients that investing in the "next big thing" is as much a retirement strategy as trying to bottle lightning as a strategy for lighting your living room. It doesn't make sense. A good investment strategy is as much about mitigating risk as it is about maximizing returns.

- Investment performance is a long-term construct. If you are reading a book to find one investment that should produce the "big win," you're probably doing the wrong thing. Unprecedented gains are about luck, not skill. I would rather focus on the skill that builds over time than rest my chances on the luck that more often than not leads to heartbreak.

- There's no such thing as a perfect pick. It may seem like Apple is a good idea or that investing all of your money into the stock of the bank you work for makes sense, but it doesn't. My batting average with the 25 companies I buy every six months that make up the 52-Week Low strategy is around .700 to .750. That means three out of every four companies on the list grow during the period I own them. This is a terrific return, well above the average. But it also means that at least one out of every four is wrong. The key is to insulate yourself from being wholly invested in one thing, be it a company or a mutual fund.

- This time is never different. If rule number one of investing is buy low, sell high, then this is rule number two. At the time I am writing this, both the Dow and the S&P are setting new record highs every day. Only a fool thinks this will continue forever. This doesn't mean the 52-Week Low is only about not losing money as opposed to making money. Quite the contrary. You'll see that the strategy consistently outperforms the market, but it doesn't always outperform the market. Sometimes the market soars to new heights, well beyond what the 52-Week Low could achieve. But what goes up must come down, and this strategy is as focused on managing the inevitable downturn and returning to profitability as quickly as possible as it is about taking advantage of large gains. Healthy skepticism protects the realistic. Not having it leaves you exposed to the risk of unintended consequences.
- There is a sharp difference between the mindset of an investor and that of a believer. The 52-Week Low is designed to take emotion as far out of the equation as possible. Emotion blinds us to opportunity and risk. The reason this strategy performs as well as it does is that it helps to take emotion out of the consideration set when making a decision. Mine. Yours. My clients'. As an investor, it's important to disassociate how you feel about a company from the likelihood that company has of making you money. I always laugh when I read a headline about someone's hope for a stock or fear of a trend. Hope and fear are not based on data, they are based on response. It may seem cold. It is not meant to be. I am not a robot. I am an emotional being, just like you and everyone you know. But I recognize the risks that go with feeling and have done my best to remove risk as much as possible.

The 52-Week Low is not a get-rich-quick scheme. I do not and will not promise huge gains. What I will do is show you how having a consistent strategic approach to recognizing opportunity and mitigating risk will benefit you and your investments. I will show you how inversion and a willingness to trust—but verify—should lead to better results. And I will encourage you to do your homework when it comes to the strategy. I have had two independent back tests of the strategy, one of which was performed going all the way back to 1980. The results have been consistent. The 52-Week Low has had a high consistency of outperforming the market in both up markets and down markets. It has mitigated permanent loss during market catastrophes and provided for fast recovery in the aftermath.

Ever since I was a kid, I've understood the value of inversing. And now I encourage you to do the same. I may be the last person I ever expected to write a book, but if I've learned one thing about life and investments, it is this: never trust what you expect. It's always better to trust what you can know.

I hope you will read the pages that follow with an open yet critical mind, because there is no such thing as certainty, particularly when it comes to investing. But after having spent half my life looking for a better way, this is the closest I believe we can come to it.

You will also notice that I don't just cover the mechanics of investing or the filters that drive the 52-Week Low formula in this book. I also cover the biases and cognitive behaviors that drive investors—too often in the wrong direction. Making good investment decisions often requires overcoming these biases and behaviors, going against instinct in pursuit of logic, and sticking with a strategy. I won't dwell too long on these, as there are a lot of great resources out there that help us understand why we make decisions the way we do. But I would be remiss if I ignored the human side of investing completely.

Finally, you will find a series of case studies based on both actual performance and independent back testing that proves the 52-Week Low to not only deliver better performance but mitigate risk and provide faster recovery after periods of great loss in the market. For a full 30-year back-testing report, contact me at **www.52weeklow.com**.

Case Study: Author Profile

Jacobian Inverse: If I want to remain mediocre and experience a life of misery, I would rather respond to the environment around me than make the effort to change my reality. I will make a habit of finding all the reasons why I am a victim. I will definitely have no interest in challenging collective wisdom, as I am just a small fish in a big pond. If I want to learn as little as possible from this book, I will not seek to understand who the author is, his or her motivation for writing the book, and what circumstances led to its creation. If the author of the book is an expert, I will not learn about how that expertise was gained. I will focus only on the words and do as little as possible to understand the meaning beyond the pages.

Who do I think I am to write this book, and what do I know about proving collective wisdom or common assumptions wrong?

It's an important question. You're going to read a lot about process and data, numbers, and analysis in the pages that follow. You're going to read my thoughts about removing emotion and emotional investment from the investing process. You're going to read about Warren Buffett and Michael Porter and dozens of other luminaries in the world of finance. You're going to read about companies that have struggled and the opportunities those struggles have created. You're going to read about cognitive biases and the forces that shape the way we make decisions. But you are going to read a little about me and my experiences that have led me to question the common wisdom and have given me the confidence to pursue the right path, not just the one trampled and trodden by those that have come before me.

And the impression that all of these things may leave is an unfounded belief that I am not a people person and that my reliance on logic and data somehow remove the humanity from the relationships I have with my clients, my family, my friends, and loved ones. This is wrong. If I have learned anything at all in more than 15 years of working in the wealth management industry, it is this: it is a relationship business.

(continued)

(continued)

The relationships you form with clients are based on your ability to create value—not just monetary value, but real value—in their lives. It's not all that different from the relationship a reader has with an author. The reader has to invest himself in the author—not just his words—in order to derive value from the book. He has to have a feeling that he understands who the author is and what makes him tick before he will lend credence to the author's thoughts, theories, or ideas.

When I'm meeting with a client for the first time, we sit down and talk about each other's lives long before we talk about business. With existing clients, the meetings follow the same pattern. I'm never comfortable ending a meeting without making a human connection. As a financial strategist and adviser, it's important that clients trust me. As a husband, it's important that my wife trusts me. As a father, it's important that my children trust me, and it's important to me that they know who I am. The same goes for my friendships and other relationships. I want them to trust me, to know me.

I want the same of you.

I want readers like you to understand who I am so that you will understand the information I'm conveying a little better. I want you to know that I'm someone who cares very deeply about my clients and considers them to be friends and family, not just a name on an account. I take that responsibility seriously. I welcome it.

This was the central point in my struggle when deciding whether to write about myself. But, with the help of some friends, I've come to realize that readers will not get as much out of this book as I hope they do without understanding a bit about me. So rather than writing a full biography or transcribing my resume, rather than bragging about success or wallowing in defeat, I thought I would start with one crucial and central question and do my best to answer it in the most relevant way possible: Who am I?

I am a man who has been very fortunate in my life to have the opportunity and mindset to challenge common beliefs. I have been able to overcome obstacles and the process of overcoming them has been integral in forming my approach to everything—life, work, relationships, and financial independence by the age of 33.

I am a big believer in challenging the status quo, of going against the grain. But I don't believe in doing so for sport. That is, I don't subscribe to the notion that simply because something is common knowledge or accepted practice, it necessarily is wrong. Rather, I take a scientific approach to life. I experiment and do so with the honest intent of challenging assumed results and creating better outcomes.

You might say that I'm the kind of person who doesn't take "no" for an answer, but I've been told "no" a lot in my life. There are times when "no" is the answer you have to accept because it is the right answer—the only answer. Instead, I'm the kind of person that doesn't accept "no" at face value. I want to understand why it is. I am curious about the ways "no" can be morphed into something different, perhaps even "yes."

I'm also not the kind of person that likes to sit still, to take the path of least resistance simply because it is less resistant. Instead, I keep challenging myself and my thinking. I challenge other people's approaches but am more than happy to accept when their approaches are simply better than mine. The only way to do this, to keep moving forward regardless of how, is to be completely and totally devoted to improvement and results.

I make no claims that my approach—to life and the 52-Week Low—is groundbreaking economic theory. In fact, it's kind of the opposite. Far from revolutionary and complex, the 52-Week Low simplifies the act of investing by removing complicating factors: emotion and biases. It focuses on the core, the purest desired results of any investor—improvement. Improvement in times of gain. Improvement in times of loss. Improved results and improved value.

When I'm sitting down with clients, the thing I want them to understand about me is that I am constantly going to question, to investigate, to find a better way forward. I do this on their behalf and with them in mind. It is not a matter of ego. It is a matter of gratitude. I am grateful that they have invested in me, both emotionally and financially, and I feel the responsibility of duty—the duty to make good decisions, to act with them in mind. I feel the same duty to you.

The fact is that there was no way I could not write this book and share it with the world. Part of me thought about keeping the 52-Week Low mindset and philosophy with only my business partner and brother, Zach, but as I think about my legacy and how I want to leave a lasting positive impact on the world, I had to follow my will and heart to ensure that sharing this became a reality. When I think about the value I bring to others, I believe it is one of hope and one of paradigm shifting. Through extensive reading/research, I have come to realize that the biggest competitor each of us faces is not external factors—it is our minds.

(continued)

(*continued*)

This book represents my life's work to date. It is a detailed study into the process and strategies that have led to my personal and professional successes. It is not intended to be the be-all, end-all of investing books, but an introduction to a new way of thinking, a different way of thinking.

Now that you know a bit more about who I am, I hope you can answer for yourself who it is I think I am to write this book. And I hope you can read it with that same understanding and appreciate the life experiences and mental makeup that made discovering and refining a strategy like the 52-Week Low not just possible but inevitable.

Foreword

Luke Wiley starts *The 52-Week Low Formula* with a personal confession that he was not the best student when he was young, so it only makes sense that, as a friend, I make a personal confession of my own: I once believed I was going be the next Warren Buffett.

As a child, I raised animals and sold them at the county fair. And with my growing savings came decisions—what to do with the money? To jumpstart my learning, my grandmother gave me a copy of Benjamin Graham's *The Intelligent Investor*, which describes the philosophy of value investing. I was 12 at the time, and instead of being overwhelmingly appreciative, I was secretly depressed I didn't get a Nintendo. Nonetheless, I read the book and loved it. I was hooked on value investing.

Over the next 10 years, I devoured books on value investing and eventually put my hard-earned knowledge to work, investing in value stocks and special situations. Part of my investing education included the finance PhD program at the University of Chicago. The first two years of the program were similar to drinking from a high-powered fire hose that spewed sometimes unintelligible information and math equations from the leading scholars in finance. It was not always the most enjoyable experience. However, I persevered and met Professor Nick Barberis, who was researching the intersection between financial economics and psychology, a growing field that has since come to be known as "Behavioral Finance." I took Professor Barberis's PhD seminar and read hundreds of academic papers on behavioral finance. Although I wasn't sure how I could apply my new knowledge, I recognized that psychology was a powerful force in truly understanding financial economics.

My research on value investing and behavioral finance led to my own co-authored book on value-investing, *Quantitative Value*. My book serves as a reminder that, (1) I will never be Buffett, and (2) combining a systematic decision process with a value investment philosophy has historically been a successful way to compound wealth over time.

In my mind, Luke Wiley's *52-Week Low Formula* has the two ingredients for success: (1) The process is systematic, and (2) the formula adheres to a value investment philosophy. Luke's mantra is to invert your analytical process and forget about home runs. Instead, he shows you an investment process that removes emotion and behavioral bias—and hits for percentages, powerful percentages. In my mind, this process gets us a closer to The Oracle of Omaha and a little further from Ben Graham's manic friend, "Mr. Market."

The quote, "Keep things as simple as possible, but no simpler," is often attributed to the great Albert Einstein. The *52-Week Low Formula* embodies this philosophy because of its elegant simplicity. Luke identifies the five fundamental factors that help investors methodically move down the field and score a touchdown. Luke is masterful in explaining how and why these five fundamental factors work over the long-haul. Just as Ben Hogan once distilled the golf swing into the book *Five Lessons: The Modern Fundamentals of Golf*, Wiley has reduced the investment process down to five fundamental factors he knows are mission-critical for investment success.

How Luke peels away the investment layers of stock selection and portfolio building is wonderful, and so easily understood. He peppers the book with stories of real companies, real victories, and real losses, to help the reader understand that success with the *52-Week Low Formula*—or any profitable investment program, for that matter—requires an investor with discipline and a focus on long-term performance.

At first, you may be as skeptical as I once was on the merits of the *52-Week Low Formula*. In academic jargon, "52-Week Low" translates as "low momentum." And as any empirical researcher can tell you, buying a portfolio of low momentum stocks is typically a sucker's bet. Nonetheless, Luke inverts the evidence on low momentum portfolios and finds great value among baskets of securities often left for dead by the broader investment and academic community. If you are like me, you will be pleasantly surprised by his formula. If you have been beating your head against the wall over-thinking security selection, as many of us often do, Luke's systematic approach for identifying high performance stocks is worth learning about. And as any great investor will tell you, investment philosophies founded on evidence, margin-of-safety, and a healthy dose of common sense are often associated with higher risk-adjusted returns over the long-haul.

Wesley R. Gray, PhD
Executive Managing Member, Empiritrage
Co-Author of *Quantitative Value*
March 11, 2014

Acknowledgments

There are many people I would like to acknowledge for their assistance in writing this book.

First and foremost, my family: To my supportive and loving wife, Melissa—You are everything to me. You, with God's grace, have played the biggest part in who I am today as a person, and specifically, who I am today as a father. To my business partner and brother, Zach, thank you for being my devil's advocate while developing this strategy. Your servant's heart and giving nature are traits that I have always admired. To my little, tall brother, Josh, for your inspiration and genuineness. To my parents, Larry and Annette Wiley, who never said that anything was impossible to achieve. Early in my childhood you encouraged me to ask the question "Why not me?" when challenged by the status quo. You demonstrated to me that life is much more fulfilling and bears much fruit when you're willing to play a positive role in the world around you rather than be a spectator sitting in the stands. My hope is that through my actions and words, I will be able to inspire others to challenge their perceptions and ask for themselves, "Why not me?"

To the leadership staff and research staff at UBS, thank you for your support and understanding, for your diligence and insight. I could not imagine writing this book while working at any other firm. UBS is indeed a special place. Thank you.

I especially want to thank my team members, Lynn, Karen, and Nick, who continuously make me look good and keep me on track. Your energy, focus, and commitment are major ingredients in the secret recipe.

I am also thankful to Tom Frank, my coworker at UBS, who connected me to Wesley Gray, PhD, author of *Quantitative Value*. Thankfully, Wes believed this strategy had merit and was kind enough to connect me with his editor, Bill Falloon at Wiley. Thank you, Bill, for seeing the value in the 52-Week Low formula. Thanks to all the staff at Wiley for your interest in helping this book be the best it can be for each and every reader.

To the thinking, inspiration, and leadership of Warren Buffett, Howard Marks, Bruce Greenwald, Haywood Kelly, Rob Knapp, James Montier, Chris Davis, Michael Porter, Bruce Berkowitz, Pat Dorsey, Seth Klarman, Daniel Kahneman, Mary Buffett, Michael Shearn, Paul Sonkin, Josh Rosenbaum, Donald Keough, and Charlie Munger—and many others— your influence has been important to so much of what I do and, though I may never have a chance to thank you in person, here is as good as any place.

To my friend and thought partner Curtis Zimmerman, who thankfully prodded me for years to write this book.

To my friend and collaborator Craig Heimbuch, I'm thankful for your friendship and for helping me smooth out the rough spots in the writing. Your partnership in this process has been priceless and I am eternally grateful.

I would also like to thank the equity analysts at Morningstar for their "Economic Moat" research. This level of research has been and will continue to be a valuable tool for us.

To the two individuals who have since passed away but whose thinking has impacted me greatly: Benjamin Graham, author of *Security Analysis* and the *Intelligent Investor*, the philosophy and mindset required to become a successful investor, and Earl Nightingale, author of *The Strangest Secret* and *Lead the Field*, the philosophy that we become what we think about.

To my clients, who have become friends and who have challenged my thinking over the years. Your willingness to think differently and to trust, but verify my assertions have been invaluable.

And to anyone I might have missed, I'm sorry, but know in my heart and my head, I am grateful.

With deep gratitude,
Luke

The 52-Week Low Formula

CHAPTER 1

The 52-Week Formula

Invert, always invert.

—Carl Gustav Jacob Jacobi

Inversion. Such a simple concept. If you have a problem to solve, consider all the solutions that won't work and, in so doing, the correct answer reveals itself. When I first came across the preceding quote from nineteenth-century German mathematician Carl Gustav Jacob Jacobi, it resonated. This way of thinking—in reverse—seemed to speak to the way I made decisions. Want to lose weight? Think of all the things that will make you fat and do the reverse. Want to be a better father? Think of the things that would turn your kids away. And Jacobi's maxim seemed most appropriate to my career in finance, particularly as it relates to investing's golden rule:

Buy low, sell high.

It's the cardinal rule of investing and, often, the most overused, underfollowed principle in the world of finance. Too often, investors do just the opposite—they buy a hot stock hoping it will get hotter and end up riding the downward slope toward a loss. These people are driven by the idea of a quick return, a profit that appeals to their sense of winning but defies logic and overwhelms their discipline.

If they aren't chasing stocks bound to lose, they invest in what they know: the path of least resistance. They rely on instinct, intuition, a familiar path, or wishful thinking, rather than doing the necessary work. And, as we've seen in books like *Unthinking* and *Thinking, Fast and Slow*, cognitive ease can be a powerful force.

This willingness to go with the status quo is the approach of System 1 thinking, as defined by Nobel-Prize winning economist Daniel Kahneman.[1] It's reactive, instinctive, and prone to following the path of least resistance. It's the kind of thinking that doesn't seek opportunities to challenge. System 2 thinking, however, takes little for granted. It is a challenging way of thinking because it requires consideration and a willingness to go against the grain, especially when the grain is going in the wrong direction. That's not to say it is purely contrary, but rather, it is devoted to purpose and making the best decisions possible—not simply the easiest decisions.

Psychologists refer to this phenomenon of two ways of thinking as the dual process theory. It means that something—a behavior, a response, a cognition—can happen in two separate and distinct ways: System 1 and System 2. Both are valid, but understanding the difference between them is important, especially in the context of an investment strategy like the 52-Week Low.

System 1 thinking is responsive and immediate. It's the kind of thinking Malcolm Gladwell covers in great detail in his bestselling book *Blink.* In System 1, we take small bits of information and extrapolate rapidly. We make quick decisions

---

[1] Daniel Kahneman, *Thinking, Fast and Slow* (New York: Farrar, Straus and Giroux, 2011).

based upon limited data. System 1 thinking is what tells you that you shouldn't walk down a dark alley; it's the way you respond in a heated conversation. It's not purely emotional, but it is emotive. When in the process of System 1 thinking, your mind is responding, firing a specific kind on neuron that makes unconscious connections. It is thinking without thinking. It's the thing that tells you to sell when you see the stock ticker on the bottom of your television screen flash negative news about a company you own. System 1 thinking is not considered thinking; rather, it is the extremely rapid thinking that keeps you safe, keeps you moving and dictates the process of getting routine things done (shaving, brushing your teeth, etc.) without having to consider every step in the process.

System 2 is just the opposite. System 2 thinking requires you to seek out input, to consider data and extrapolate consequences. Where System 1 is spontaneous, System 2 is more academic. System 2 thinking is how we process context and overcome cognitive biases to make informed decisions. A System 2 thinker—and we are all capable of both kinds of thinking—considers the costs and benefits of walking down that alley. In System 2, we don't respond in the heated conversation, but walk away to consider what we really want to say. We see the stock ticker at the bottom of the screen as another source of data or as an impetus to seek more information. System 2 thinking is how we make plans to change our routines and project the long-term benefit of something.

The 52-Week Low is heavily System 2. The strategy is based on formulating long-term decisions based on many consistent data points. System 1 is recognizing an opportunity to make a quick buck, while System 2—and the 52-Week Low—is about making good decisions to build wealth.

System 1 investing follows preset rules, discourages critical thought, and makes it easy for investors to follow preset paths. It takes minimal effort to buy a mutual fund with the notion that the more acronyms a money manager has behind his name (CFA, MBA, PhD), the better the results. Not exactly. These mutual funds are relatively familiar and don't require a lot of thought, in their mind, so they go that route even when the evidence doesn't support it. Many individuals and investors don't take the time to do their homework or challenge their belief system. Instead, they read surface-level articles and follow their emotions and often end up buying into something that is already at or around its high. For all of us, it is much more comfortable emotionally to invest in a mutual fund, index fund, or stock that looks healthy and is favored by Wall Street. We all have this bias in some form, called the *conformity bias*, and it is one that can severely impact your financial health. Three quarters of all mutual funds underperform their respective benchmarks over a 10-year period, and yet behavior doesn't change.[2]

It didn't take me that long to figure out that something was wrong. Maybe not wrong, but certainly not right. I was in my 20s, a young financial adviser working for a big company, attracting new clients and making the kinds of recommendations I was supposed to make—mutual funds of every shape and size. But it felt off. I was doing my job and doing it well. My clients seemed content, but I knew there was a better way. What really opened my eyes was when the stock of the world's largest consumer products company, Procter & Gamble, dropped, and six Wall Street analysts downgraded the stock on March 7, 2000, after the stock had dropped approximately 50 percent. A funny thing happened. One of my clients called me after P&G had fallen off the proverbial cliff and said they would like to buy some shares. I remember telling them that six analysts had downgraded the stock, including the firm I was working for at the time. The

[2]See www.forbes.com/sites/richardfinger/2013/04/15/five-reasons-your-mutual-fund-probably-underperforms-the-market/; www.businessinsider.com/84-mutual-funds-underperform-2012-3; and https://pressroom.vanguard.com/nonindexed/7.5.2013_The_bumpy_road_to_outperformance.pdf.

client persisted and said, "Buy it." So I bought it thinking they were going to regret it, and instead their investment made a considerable amount of money as the stock rose in value.

What I realized is that most analysts will upgrade a stock after it has become common knowledge that the antibiotics have worked and the stock has recovered, and will downgrade a stock after it has become common knowledge the company is ill and the recent stock performance is underwhelming.

Where do you have the most risk as an investor? Buying a business that everyone already likes, where enthusiasm is high among investors and Wall Street analysts, and that is trading around its 52-Week High? Or buying a business that no one really likes, where enthusiasm is low among investors and Wall Street analysts, and that is trading around its 52-Week Low?

Hint: A company that has had really good recent performance has not made you any money. It has made money for those who already own the stock. You would be putting in new money. A company that has had a really underwhelming recent performance has not lost you any money. It has lost money for those who already own it. So, which one should you buy? Which one do most investors buy?

Remember: If you were truly trying to buy low, then wouldn't the headlines, analyst recommendations, and investor enthusiasm be pretty underwhelming?

If you were truly trying to sell high, then wouldn't the headlines, analyst recommendations, and investor enthusiasm be pretty overwhelming?

In his book *The Little Book of Behavioral Investing*,[3] James Montier explores the folly of forecasting. It seems that, as humans, we just aren't very good at it. Economists have failed to predict the last four recessions, he writes, and investment analysts are staggeringly wrong—two-year forecasts are wrong

---

[3]James Montier, *The Little Book of Behavioral Investing: How Not to Be Your Own Worst Enemy* (Hoboken, NJ: Wiley, 2010).

94 percent of the time, and even 12-month forecasts have a miss rate of 45 percent.

It's worth keeping this in mind the next time you listen to a news report about the state of the American economy or a friend or advisor gives you advice based on a long-term forecast. So why, then, do we all fall in line?

Well, it's human nature to want to know the future, to desire the comfort of foresight. But it's a human failing to rely upon someone's prediction. We like to trust people in authority or people who we perceive as having more credibility than we do, more experience, more education. The simple fact remains, however, that no one knows what the future holds. No one. So isn't it better to make decisions based upon what you can know—the present and the past?

I've never been one of those people to fall in line. I grew up in a military family, bouncing from city to city, base to base. I was an athlete, but I don't think I've ever been a jock. I had the discipline to get better and better at the things I set my eyes on, the focus and drive to not rest until I did, and an innate understanding that relying on other people to shape my self-esteem and confidence didn't make much sense. Maybe it was because I was the new kid a lot. Maybe it was something my parents showed me by example. Maybe it's just who I am.

These qualities, I have come to realize, are the ones I admire in other people. My parents, Larry and Annette; Napoleon Hill; Nelson Mandela; Abraham Lincoln; and investors I admire like Howard Marks, Chris Davis, Charlie Munger, Seth Klarman, Bruce Greenwald, Bruce Berkowitz, and Joel Greenblatt. They don't follow the herd in order to fit in. They have the kind of fortitude and integrity I've always aspired to.

That's why I made a decision to explore a different path. There's a lot of success to be had and money to be made as a financial adviser promoting the latest mutual fund. But, for me, success is not measured solely by money. Instead, I knew that if I wanted to look at my work and feel a sense of accomplishment, I needed to follow my instinct and look for a better path forward, a different kind of investing that relied heavily on a set of rules and principles derived from logic, not sales sheets, and required discipline to outgain the average and deliver better results for clients.

I think I first realized that there was a better way when I was in my 20s, working for a big financial services firm and toeing the common line. I sold the mutual funds and followed the advice given by our analysts. But I was never comfortable with the idea that wealth management should be about doing what everyone else is doing.

This blind faith in what is being prescribed by the consensus of Wall Street experts breeds the kind of comfort that leads to complacency and an illogical and fictional sense of fear of doing things any other way. There are countless studies that show it is very dangerous to your wealth to follow the advice of the "consensus," no matter how impressive the credentials.[4] But I think the quote in the front matter from economist and author John Kenneth Galbraith sums it up pretty well: "The function of economic forecasting is to make astrology look respectable."[5]

In fact, I recently read a study[6] that tracked the forecasting accuracy from the *Wall Street Journal* Survey of Economists regarding the 6-month average forecasted interest rate direction versus the actual direction of interest rates from December 1982 to December 2012. These economists were asked if interest rates over the next 6 months would be up or down. How accurate were their forecasts? The forecast was

---

[4]See Meb Faber, "The Folly of Forecasting," www.mebfaber.com/2010/03/01/the-folly-of-forecasting.

[5]Quoted in Nassim Taleb, *Fooled by Randomness: The Hidden Role of Chance in Life and in the Markets* (New York: Random House, 2005).

[6]Davis Advisors, "The Wisdom of Great Investors," http://davisfunds.com/downloads/WGI.pdf.

incorrect 64 percent of the time. Remember—these economists were not asked what the 30-year treasury rate or 10-year treasury rate would be in 6 months, but merely whether the rate would be higher or lower in 6 months. They were right only 36 percent of the time.

Why do we continue to follow the experts? Not only is it cognitive ease—being lazy and not doing our homework—but it is also another type of subconscious thinking, called the *halo effect*. The halo effect is quite prominent in most of our decision making. It is how we perceive those with whom we interact. Wall Street analysts, the investment community, and all of us have to be mindful of the halo effect. Phil Rosenzweig, writing for McKinsey & Company, explains the halo effect this way:

> Imagine a company that is doing well, with rising sales, high profits, and a sharply increasing stock price. The tendency is to infer that the company has a sound strategy, a visionary leader, motivated employees, an excellent customer orientation, a vibrant culture, and so on. But when that same company suffers a decline—if sales fall and profits shrink—many people are quick to conclude that the company's strategy went wrong, its people became complacent, it neglected its customers, its culture became stodgy, and more. In fact, these things may not have changed much, if at all. Rather, company performance, good or bad, creates an overall impression— a halo—that shapes how we perceive its strategy, leaders, employees, culture, and other elements.[7]

In addition, if you study the stock performance of companies known as glamour stocks versus the stock performance of

---

[7]Phil Rosenzweig, "The halo effect and other managerial delusions," *McKinsey Quarterly*, February 2007, www.mckinsey.com/insights/strategy/the_halo_effect_and_other_managerial_delusions.

companies known as despised stocks, who do you think comes out ahead?

We assume the glamour stocks do, because it is our confirmation bias that tells us that the more expensive stocks are the better performers. In reality, it is often the despised stocks that represent the best opportunity for growth. And it is not just stocks where this bias plays out. Think of the last time you were standing in the grocery store aisle, looking at detergents. Without a pre-established preference, how would you make the decision of which detergent performs the best? Well, packaging may be an influence, but more than likely, you assume the most expensive product is the most effective. It makes sense, right? But it is more than likely wrong-headed because the products are probably all made of the same chemicals and have similar effectiveness. James Montier makes a similar argument and comparison with painkillers, branded products versus unbranded, in his study on the placebo effect and glamour stocks.[8] Subjects who paid more for their painkillers reported less pain, even when they were given a placebo, than those who paid less. It's a bias against "cheapness," as he calls it, but it is really a sign of how we are programmed—in System 1, anyway—to defer to price as a measure of quality, how we make decisions based on incomplete or misleading data.

I was successful the old way, but it wasn't until I began critically reviewing the system that I began to understand what fulfillment looked like. I absorbed the work of other investment strategy leaders. I studied how the people who have been most successful in building and maintaining their wealth did so, and before long I was working on an approach all my own.

The Birth of The 52-Week Low from a $1,400 Book

So I started doing the work—reading everything I could and working through the math—until the truth began to reveal itself.

---

[8]James Montier, "Mind Matters," Societe Generale, March 10, 2008, www.designs .valueinvestorinsight.com/bonus/bonuscontent/docs/Montier_Cheapness_Bias.pdf.

It all came together from one sentence within a $1,400 book. The 52-Week Low focus spoke to me when I read Seth Klarman's book, *Margin of Safety: Risk-Averse Value Investing Strategies for the Thoughtful Investor*. In the chapter titled "The Challenge of Finding Attractive Investments," he stated, "Looking at stocks on the *Wall Street Journal*'s leading percentage-decline and new-low lists, for example, occasionally turns up an out-of-favor investment idea." This solidified my hunting ground. I would evaluate businesses that are trading close to their 52-Week Low. And by degrees, I came to see the answer, and it had been right in front of me the entire time: the 52-Week Low.

Believe it or not, the 52-Week Low list that had been recommended as fertile investment soil popped up again on page 397 of *The Intelligent Investor, Revised Edition*, in the paragraph titled, "Looking Under the Right Rocks."

> Unlike most people, many of the best professional investors first get interested in a company when its share price goes down, not up. Christopher Browne of Tweedy Brown Global Value Fund, William Nygren of the Oakmark Fund, Robert Rodriguez of FPA Capital Fund, and Robert Torray of the Torray Fund all suggest looking at the daily list of the new 52-week lows in the *Wall Street Journal* or the similar table in the "Market Week" section of *Barron's*. That will point you toward stocks and industries that are unfashionable or unloved and that thus offer the potential for high returns once perceptions change.

The 52-Week Low is the antithesis of System 1 thinking. It is measured, considered, constantly challenged, and disciplined in such a way to account for and avoid cognitive bias and emotion-based decision making. It is a System 2 approach to identifying investments with real opportunities.

Even the best companies in the world—names you know, products you use—go through periods of contraction. Their stock falls, their rate of growth slows, but they are fundamentally sound. In my opinion, these companies going through this kind of cycle or struggle represent the best opportunity for a disciplined investor looking to make smart decisions that have been proven to beat market averages.

It's not all that different from "Moneyball," the System 2 statistical approach to fielding a baseball team profiled in Michael Lewis's popular book of the same name. The Oakland A's needed to compete on the field but were unable to compete with the big budgets of other teams. So they looked at tried-and-true players, the ones with long records of particular kinds of success. Even if they are beaten up, injured, or aging, their record speaks for itself. Don't focus on the players on a hot streak; look for the ones with a track record of success.

I've spent years refining the principles behind 52-Week Low, back-testing data, putting my own money on the line, and the results have been impressive. My clients—those willing to take a slightly different approach to investing their retirement dollars—have never been happier.

The 52-Week Low, when you look at it on paper, seems so simple. Almost too simple. We look at companies and judge them based on five basic questions:

1. Do they have a durable competitive advantage?

   Are they the kind of company that is hard to compete with, either because they have cornered a difficult market or because competing with them would require an unreasonably high investment by others?

2. What is the purchase value of the company relative to its free cash flow?

   If someone were to come in and buy the entire company, would the free cash flow being generated be well in excess of simply investing in a 10-year Treasury bond? After all, the cash flow on a 10-year Treasury bond is said to be "risk-free" while the free cash flow from a company is not without risk.

3. What's the return on invested capital of the company?

Is the company using its money wisely to create returns greater than its cost of capital, or is it destroying shareholder value due to generating returns below its cost of capital? Is it using its money well to create returns, or is it taking on bad investments that don't pay off?

4. Can it pay off its long-term debt quickly with free cash flow?

There are a lot of companies out there that are making a lot of money, but should revenues stall or decelerate, could their long-term debt be paid off within a short period with free cash flow?

5. Finally, is it trading close to its 52-Week Low?

The 52-Week Low formula is based on the idea that even the best companies go through a skid, a downturn in stock value. This is the key ingredient to the strategy because you are buying into a business that is more than likely or completely out of favor with the investing public and Wall Street analysts. Is it better to buy a good business trading at an attractive valuation, where capital is scarce; or is it better to buy a good business that is overvalued, where there is an abundance of capital? Which investment choice would feel most comfortable emotionally? A quote I share with clients is, "If an investment feels really good emotionally to buy, then you may be paying too much for the business." To paraphrase Warren Buffett, "You want to do business with Mr. Market when he is very depressed and giving away his inventory and turn your back when he is excited and wanting to do business with you." *Reminder:* We don't just buy any company trading closest to its 52-Week Low; we buy good businesses at attractive valuations that are trading near their 52-Week Lows. The five filters—which will be detailed throughout this book—are in place to ensure that the company in question has more of a mild infection versus a terminal disease, whereby over time the antibiotics should kick in.

It is about buying the "right business" at its 52-Week Low versus buying "any business" at its 52-Week Low. If it is the wrong business or it is a business that operates in an industry with poor economics (e.g., the steel industry), then there is a high probability that that company will continue to reset its 52-Week Low and you could permanently lose your investment.

The 52-Week Low is a strategic way of narrowing down the wide world of possibility when it comes to investing by starting with an end goal—outperforming the market, with less downside risk—and working backwards. It is a logic-based, disciplined approach to narrowing down the 3,000 publicly traded companies in the market to the 25 that represent the best opportunity for creating real value in the coming months (Figure 1.1).

In developing these key questions, these sequential filters, I realized I was on to something. I felt energized, like I was finally using the part of me that always knew there was a better way forward. You will see later in the book I truly was trying to find ways to disprove the strategy. I had to be willing to apply my own skepticism to my own formula. In backtesting the formula to either approve or disprove it, my thinking was proven correct, as shown by the empirical proof shared throughout the chapters and case studies in this book. When you understand the preceding five questions, it becomes pretty clear why it works: good companies. Think about it: when a good business that operates in a good industry with good economics finds a cliff to fall off of, rarely does it find another cliff to fall off of. In fact, most of these types of businesses correct their mistakes and begin their ascension again. Let's take a look at Procter & Gamble, the world's leading household product manufacturer, specifically what happened on March 7, 2000. The stock dropped 30 percent in 24 hours. The company with more than 20 billion-dollar brands. Guess how many Wall Street analysts downgraded the stock

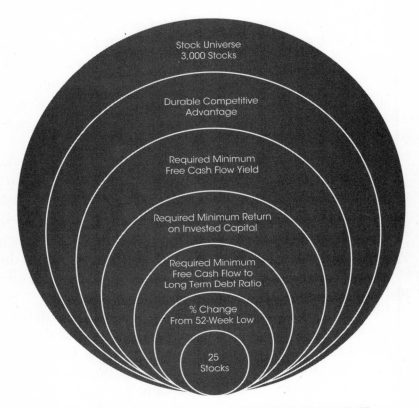

Figure 1.1   The 52-Week Low and the Wide World of Possibility

after it had already dropped? Six firms downgraded the stock on March 7, 2000 (see Table 1.1).

Guess where the stock was trading six months later? Twelve months later? Five years later?

You will find a similar occurrence in many of the 52-Week Low stocks, as each business more often than not has been downgraded or is not a fan favorite of Wall Street. To paraphrase Matthew McLennan of First Eagle Funds, where there is a high degree of enthusiasm, there is also a high degree of risk. Once again it sounds counterintuitive, but remember: "Return on investment is typically the highest where capital is scarce," according to Richard Bernstein, CEO of Richard Bernstein Advisors. I would also add that where there is an abundance of capital and

Table 1.1   Wall Street Firms that Downgraded the Stock After It Had Already Dropped

			From	To
7-Mar-00	Banc of America Securities	Downgrade	Strong Buy	Buy
7-Mar-00	Credit Suisse First Boston	Downgrade	Buy	Hold
7-Mar-00	Donaldson, Lufkin & Jenrette	Downgrade	Top Pick	Market Perform
7-Mar-00	JP Morgan	Downgrade	Buy	LT Buy
7-Mar-00	Merrill Lynch	Downgrade	NT Accum	NT Neutral
7-Mar-00	Morgan Stanley Dean Witter	Downgrade	Outperform	Neutral

Source: Yahoo! Finance.

euphoria, there is a high probability of financial loss and the return on investment is typically the lowest.

If you combine sound investing principles and a disciplined, logic-based approach that eliminates the frailty of fear, the indecision of emotion, and the transience of fad, you get a clearer picture of how the market should perform, how investing should be done. The reason this formula is timeless is that the investing public and most of Wall Street suffer from investing myopia. Their time frame for a company is 30 to 90 days, and when the short-term outlook looks dire, millions to billions of dollars flee the company, which creates opportunity for the 52-Week Low investor. Table 1.2 shows a list of businesses that you will not believe were ever hated and despised by Wall Street—and it wasn't too long ago. Believe it or not, I could list pages upon pages of stocks illustrating this point.

Once again, I have to ask—what do you think the investor sentiment was like around the businesses listed in Table 1.2 after their stocks fell off the proverbial cliff? What do you think the public sentiment is like now for these same businesses? Would you buy them now, or would you sell them now?

Table 1.2 Companies Once "Hated" by Wall Street

	Current Price*
Starbucks at $7.83, November 21, 2008	$77.21
McDonalds at $12.82, March 7, 2003	$96.38
Disney at $15.83, March 6, 2009	$76.34
Pfizer at $14.44, June 25, 2010	$30.74
Johnson & Johnson at $58.57, March 18, 2011	$94.29
Wal-Mart at $49.75, August 12, 2011	$78.45
Best Buy at $11.29, December 28, 2012	$38.38
NetApp at $27.34, November 9, 2012	$40.82
Western Union at $11.95, November 2, 2012	$17.44

*Yahoo! Finance closing price as of January 7, 2014.

Popular opinion said the same things emotional investors were thinking: Stay away! Don't buy! The MBAs from Harvard and the PhDs from Yale were saying to sit on the sidelines. We need to be careful to think for ourselves and not get blinded by the halo effect as well as cognitive ease. We must not be lazy in our thinking.

Do you listen to them, or do you have a formula that helps you apply rational thinking and logic and buy them?

Cognitively, it is a lot easier to agree and listen to noise, when in reality the correct answer was—and often is—to buy. Companies, far from being dead on arrival, are more than likely suffering from a cold, but are being left for dead by popular opinion. Store closings, expense cuts, market clarity, leadership changes—all the kinds of indicators that send gut investors running for the hills. All the while, the formula serves to avoid those companies that are trying to hide a terminal illness: high levels of debt, an industry with poor economics, a history of destroying shareholder value, and so on.

Investing and managing money doesn't have to be a mystery. Nor does it have to feel like a guessing game. I realized this early on in my career, and it all began with Jacobi and his maxim, which changed the way I approach not only investing, but every aspect of my life.

Invert. Always invert.

A somewhat obscure nineteenth-century mathematician, Carl Gustav Jacob Jacobi was the first Jewish mathematician appointed as a professor to a German university. Born in the Kingdom of Prussia in 1804, his work changed the way mathematics was studied. And it all boils down to those three words: "Invert. Always invert."

What does it mean? Well, it's almost so simple that it defies reason. Jacobi advocated that, when it comes to problem solving, we start by understanding the desired outcome and then identify all the factors that will ensure it can't be reached. Through the process of identifying the ways we won't succeed and eliminating them, what are we left with? The building blocks of a strategy for success.

I use Jacobi constantly. I have even applied this level of thinking within my marriage. When I was getting married to my lovely wife, I considered all the things that would lead to an unsuccessful marriage—infidelity, intemperance, disregard, and so on—and promised myself not to do those things. When it comes to physical fitness, I identified all the things that wouldn't make me healthy and eliminated them from my life.

Too often, we are looking for secret solutions. We look for those things that will get us to the top when we should be looking for and avoiding the things that will take us to the bottom or, worse, leave us where we are. By inversing the way we approach problems, we don't need to figure out the "secret"; we simply need to avoid the pitfalls.

This approach to problem solving has been invaluable in my life, my career, my relationships, and my well-being. It is also the basis of everything you are about to read in this book. Each chapter will begin with an application of Jacobi's logic and outline the sure factors that will detract from a successful investment strategy as they pertain to the 52-Week Low filter covered in that chapter. These are meant to be shorthand, to lend context to the thinking and reveal the approach that led to the development of the filter and the strategy as a whole.

I encourage you to do the same thing with everything you are about to read. Inverse my own thinking and approach. Do your own homework. Formulate your own approach. I know I've tried. I'm constantly trying to shoot holes in the 52-Week Low formula, but it has consistently outperformed even my most ardent attempts to find its flaws. Still, this is not about blind faith or taking my word for it. Back-test the approach. Research the flaws in my logic. I'd love to know what you come up with. Contact me at **www.52weeklow.com** if you come up with something.

2

Herding and the Bandwagon Effect

If you want to achieve above average outcomes you must be willing to take an unconventional approach. If your approach is conventional and commonly used then you guarantee average results.

—Howard Marks, *The Most Important Thing: Uncommon Sense for the Thoughtful Investor*

Jacobian Inverse: I would prefer to invest alongside the masses to ensure I achieve average results. It feels comfortable, as there is safety in numbers. I realize there is no use to thinking differently than the investing public, as it is much easier emotionally to be one of many versus one of few. We will all win and lose together.

The feeling that there's safety in numbers goes back to our most primal, instinctive roots. Early man found safety in tribes—literally, safety from predators, famine, and deprivation. And this instinct has carried through time, changes in behavior, and cultures. As a species, we have developed from primitive bands of hunters and gatherers to modern tech-forward explorers of worlds both real and virtual. Still, we have not evolved beyond the herd mentality. If we see an empty restaurant during the dinner rush, we assume there's something wrong with it. If we see people flocking to another, our instincts tell us it must be good.

There's ease in herding—emotional, behavioral, cognitive, and otherwise. It's System 1 thinking. We have an instinct to belong, something described by behavioral scientists as the *Bandwagon Effect,* a term first used in 1848 by popular clown, entertainer, and political activist Dan Rice. The concept of the bandwagon is part of our language, our culture, and our politics. We encourage people to join our movements, our causes, our candidates, by telling them to get on the bandwagon. Depending on our point of view, being on the bandwagon can mean being among the popular, the smart set. Or, as the presidential candidate William Jennings Bryan used the term, it can be derogatory, a negative term for the complacent majority.

In 1951, Swarthmore College psychologist Solomon Asch began a series of experiments to understand the influence a crowd can have on an individual's decision-making. In one experiment, seven male students were shown a card with a single line drawn on it. Then they were shown a second card with three lines—each of different lengths—on it and asked to say which line was the same length as the one on the original card. All seven students were introduced as participants. All were seated in the same room and could hear the other participants' responses.

But in reality, only one of the students was an actual participant. The other six were a part of the team conducting the study. The test would be given three times. The first two times, the members of the team were instructed to give the correct answer. For the last one, they all gave an incorrect answer. And in all cases, the sole true participant was seated in such a way that he or she would give an answer last.

To control his results, Asch recruited 87 "real" participants. Fifty followed the format above—sitting in the room with the six other "participants," hearing the other answers first, and giving their answers last. The other 37 participants were given the test alone in a room with no other people to influence their answers.

What do you think happened?

According to results Asch later published,[1] the influence of the crowd is profound and disturbing.

The control group performed as expected. Of the 37 participants, the number of incorrect answers given to the question was less than one percent of the total answers given. When left alone to make a considered decision, people generally choose correctly. But what about the 50 participants influenced by a band of confederates?

They performed distinctly worse.

Twenty-five percent never gave an incorrect answer, despite the influence of the group. But 75 percent, a full three-quarters of the participants, gave at least one incorrect response.

Why? Because the bandwagon effect plays into our instincts to conform, to be a part of the herd.

In general, herding is a good thing. This isn't to say we need conformity—far from it. Nor is it to say that outliers can't inspire us. But, in general, we seek comfort in each other, and this is positive, except for one place—investments, where joining a pack can defeat one of the core principles that every successful investor lives by: buy low and sell high.

Herds, bands of investors gathered around the comforting warmth of a hot stock, end up driving prices up beyond intrinsic value. Those early to the game benefit, but the late ones? Well, they buy high, and after the stock begins to return to its actual value, they end up selling low.

If herds provide comfort and peace of mind, going against the grain requires overcoming basic human instinct. We're born to think, "Everyone else is doing it, so why shouldn't I?" But, as investors, we should be thinking, "Everyone else is doing it; there's no reason I should, too."

---

[1] Solomon Asch, "Studies of Independence and Conformity: A Minority against a Unanimous Majority," *Psychological Monographs*, 1956

What are the stock market and the investment industries if not a giant, multi-chambered room with other people in it? After all, nearly all the information we are given about investments is based upon trends—trends set by the herd, by the folks on the bandwagon. Apple's stock has doubled? Well, that's not because of an individual, but millions of individuals agreeing on its value based on the rising price. The rising price is based on millions buying. How is that so different from sitting in a room with six other people and listening to their answers about the length of the line? It's not. And it's human nature—particularly if the herd has gotten it right some of the time—to assume the herd offers us safety.

It does not.

Warren Buffett, whose reputation as a genius investor needs no description here, has made fortune after fortune by observing trends, identifying tribes, and running away from them. When everyone else is running from the railroads, he doubles down. When people are running toward tech, he looks to industrial conglomerates. Is he just a contrarian? Does he have a super-secret scientific method? Is he psychic?

No. Warren Buffett and all mega-successful investors like him understand that making money in the market is just as much a study in human nature as it is in stock valuation. He watches people and looks for the overlooked. He observes trends and tribes and looks the other way for opportunities that run counter to human nature. He has an approach, to be sure, and metrics he uses to judge the real value of a stock—not just its trading value—but uses the herding mentality to filter the lines in his book.

This isn't, of course, to say that popularity is a quantitative measure. It's not, and that's the point. Popularity is merely a reflection of trend, not a measure of real worth. Investing, at least the 52-Week Low strategy of investing, is based on that which can be measured—data, quantitative analysis that reveals intrinsic value, not just implied or inferred value.

Here's how the fallacy of popularity plays out.

Imagine that there are two stocks. One is growing at a breakneck pace and has been for months. It's a technology stock, an e-retail company led by a visionary CEO who aims to change the definition of modern-day logistics. He is investing like crazy in new facilities, new tracking measurement systems, new ways of doing one of the oldest business activities in the world. The other is a bricks-and-mortar retailer that has been around for decades. This company was once the talk of the investment town, but it is no longer shiny and new. It is old. It represents an old way of buying and selling goods. The bloom, as they say, is off the rose from a popular sentiment perspective, and the company's stock price has slid to a recent record low.

Why? Well, the first company has become a part of the popular lexicon. It is constantly in the news. Its CEO is a celebrity who graces the covers of magazines. He has built a network of popular support that has led to a stock price that seems headed in only one direction.

No one knows the name of the other CEO, and when you drive by the stores in suburban strip malls, you get a sense of both nostalgia and sadness. Remember when you used to shop that way? Remember when that seemed like a good idea?

What if I told you those two companies were Amazon and Best Buy? How would you feel about that? You would, like so many people, gravitate toward Amazon. It seems intuitive. It seems like the direction the world is going. And based on the stock price, it seems like a justified investment. In the period between October 31, 2012, and October 31, 2013, Amazon's stock rose from $232.89 per share to $364.03. That's 56 percent in growth in 12 months—an excellent return for the millions trying to get in on the action.

Surely popular opinion is justified, right?

Maybe. But what if I told you that in the exact same time period, Best Buy's stock went from $15.21 per share to $42.80, growing 181 percent? How does popular opinion factor in there? I will cover what happened with Best Buy in greater detail later in the book, but I use it here to illustrate how popular opinion—herding—often hides real opportunity.

Value-investing strategies, like Buffett's and the 52-Week Low, are not about being contrarian for the sake of being contrarian. It's not about bucking common wisdom as an act of rebellion, but for seeing popular opinion for what it actually is—something that can't be quantified in real terms to reveal opportunity—and taking a data-centric, disciplined approach to identifying investment opportunities where few others are looking for them.

Herding can be a great thing. It's a way to stay safe and warm, a way to choose a restaurant or a movie, a way to pick a vacation spot. But when it comes to investing, look for opportunities to stand alone. If you're smart about how you do it, the herds will come, and then, and only then, will you be in a position to truly buy low and sell high.

Avoiding the pitfalls of the bandwagon or the herd requires System 2 thinking. It requires us to make considered decisions as individuals based on criteria we set and rigidly adhere to. It's tempting to look at a rising stock and take the crowd's word for it, especially because we've all heard stories about people making money from that kind of situation. But doing so is wrong. We cannot let market trends be the deciding factor in our investments. We must have the courage, the wherewithal, to be focused and make independent decisions.

You have to have a measuring stick to know how long the line on the first card is and you have to be willing—if not enthusiastic—to go against the group when you know they are wrong. It's not a matter of being contrary; it's a matter of having a system and process in place to reinforce that you're doing the right thing. That's what the 52-Week Low is for, to give you the confidence in your decisions to look where others are not, to overcome the System 1 bandwagon effect and focus instead on a disciplined approach to making good decisions.

CHAPTER 3

Filter 1: Competitive Advantage

When a management with a reputation for brilliance tackles a business with a reputation for bad economics, it is the reputation of the business that remains intact.

—Warren Buffett

Jacobian Inverse: *If I wanted a high probability of losing my invested capital, I would look for industries where there is poor economics, low barriers to entry, lack of customer loyalty, and readily available alternatives. I want to find businesses where the customer has all the control and the only unique value from the business is that it offers the lowest price with no margin.*

This brings us to the correct answer—study industries that are known to have good economics, high barriers to entry, customer loyalty, and limited alternatives.

Unlike man, not every industry is created equal, which in turn means not every company is created equal.

One of the keys to value investing with the 52-Week Low formula is understanding economics. Not simple economics like the kind you learned in high school, but industry economics—the forces that shape and influence a company's profitability, sustainability, and potential for growth. Good economics is vital. Long before we ever get to a balance sheet, returns on invested capital, long-term debt to free cash flow, or any of the other company-specific filters that dictate those that either make it into the formula or don't, we look at the industry economic forces that are at work.

This first filter helps to determine those companies with a durable competitive advantage in their industries from those susceptible to industry pressures that may make it hard for them to recover, thrive, and prosper.

Warren Buffett and others have long held strong beliefs that earnings potential from investing in undervalued companies rests almost solely on the economics of the industry that company is in. Strong economics means a company has a durable competitive advantage that will help safeguard it from the kinds of competitive forces that will prevent an undervalued company from ever achieving or sustaining profitability.

So important are industry economics that Buffett and others, like me, won't even look at a company without first understanding its industry and where it fits into that industry. It doesn't matter how brilliant the management team is or how much investment it is putting into its future; if the economics don't add up, walk away.

Durable competitive advantages—or competitive moats, as they are sometimes called—give companies the ability to adjust to a changing world, fend off upstart competition, and insulate themselves from price-driven competition, daunting supply-side pressures, and overly empowered customers with the ability to dictate price through readily available access to alternatives, low switching costs, and ease of market entry. All of these things require a lot of history. It's difficult to know what kind of moat a relatively young company has. Particularly difficult is understanding how competitive forces will influence profitability without knowing how this young company will respond to competition. That's why it's generally established companies that pass this first filter in the 52-Week Low formula—ones with a history of combating or responding to changes in technology, consumer demand, and global logistics.

Some people thought I was crazy when I told them I liked the economics of Western Union. They listened when I told them I was putting money into what, to many, seemed like an old company with an old model. After all, can't you just send money over the Internet these days? And the answer is that, yes, there are ways to do it. But Western Union was a company way ahead of its time, or else perfectly adaptable to the time we are living in.

While Western Union has long been a payment logistics company, it has spent decades developing a very deep, very formidable global economic moat. Western Union handles roughly 15 percent (and growing)[1] of all foreign money transfers, with offices in hundreds of countries and cities around the world. While for many of us Western Union was once a safe and reliable way to send money to stranded travelers or ensure safe transfer of funds, it was preparing itself for a trend often overlooked in terms of economics in this country: the influx of foreign workers to the American economy. Say what you might about the politics associated with it, but the economics of immigrant workers coming to the United States to find work means long-term growth and gain for Western Union. Every time a worker saves up some cash to send home to relatives, he or she requires the services of this iconic and global company. Western Union is unique among payment

---

[1] See www.forbes.com/sites/hilarykramer/2013/05/10/wu-stock-report/.

logistics companies for its broad infrastructure and is protected in large part due to the nature of its business. While it may be easy to log on to your computer and buy something from a store using a credit card or transfer balances from one account to another, there is not a smartphone or laptop on the planet that can spit out cash. In fact, it is my understanding there are 2 billion people in the world who do not have a bank account. This is a good thing for Western Union.

Western Union deals in the logistics of cash. If anything, far from being a force in the downfall of Western Union, the digital revolution has improved its ability to do business. Transfers are instant. Tracking is intuitive. Results are guaranteed.

But before we get too far into specific examples of companies with strong competitive advantages, let's take a look at the principles that guide and define the forces at work in competitive moats.

The Five Competitive Forces

In 2008, *Harvard Business Review* published a paper by economist Michael Porter detailing how competitive forces shape the economics that determine whether a company has an advantage. The paper, called "The Five Competitive Forces that Shape Strategy," updated an article he wrote in 1979, and began: "You know that to sustain long-term profitability you must respond strategically to competition."[2]

Those five forces are:

1. Threat of New Entrants
2. Bargaining Power of Buyers
3. Threat of Substitute Products or Services
4. Bargaining Power of Suppliers
5. Rivalry among Existing Competitors

---

[2]Michael Porter, "The Five Competitive Forces that Shape Strategy," *Harvard Business Review* 86, no. 1 (January 2008): 78–93.

Porter and others argue that competition is often viewed too narrowly by investment strategists. They think only of industry rivals. Pepsi's competition is Coke. American Airlines' competition is Delta. Nike's competition is Reebok and Under Armour. McDonald's competition is Burger King, Wendy's, and other chains. This is true, of course. Industry rivalry is a form of competition, but it is by no means the only competitive force that affects a company's economics. In the same paper, Porter, who is considered by many to be among the visionary economists of his time, identifies no fewer than four other competitive forces that act on companies, all of which—whether strong or benign—represent the key components of a company's economic moats, the protective economic structures that help ensure long-term profitability.

First, let's understand established industry rivalry and its impact on competitive advantage. The forces of existing rivalry manifest themselves in several forms:

- *Discounting.* When rivals attempt to gain advantage over one another by discounting prices on comparable goods or services.
- *New product offerings.* When rivals seek advantage through innovation that gives them a temporary point of differentiation in offerings.
- *Service improvements.* When rivals attempt to take an advantage by offering service beyond the product offering. Here, think about loyalty programs that offer discounts, rewards, or services to existing or new consumers.
- *Advertising.* When rivals try to capture a stronghold in the attention and awareness among consumers and target groups.

Porter argues that such existing rivalry, in and of itself, is not a bad thing. After all, competition is the breeding ground for innovation. But the intensity and basis of such rivalries can create problematic industry economic conditions.

If, for example, rivalry is based solely on price offering to the end consumer for nearly identical goods or services and the switching cost for consumers is low, then price pressures will continue to diminish profit potential for the industry as a whole. The airline industry, particularly in the past 15 years, since the advent of Internet booking capabilities, has suffered extensively from this kind of price-based rivalry, wreaking havoc on industry economics. Consumers have been trained to seek the best deal when booking an airline ticket, regardless of airline. They seek the best price to get them where they are going. Since the travel experience for most passengers doesn't differ all that greatly from airline to airline, airlines are forced to try to underbid one another for customers, reducing the profitability of not only the individual airline but the industry as a whole. Steel producers also suffer from this sort of sea-of-sameness phenomenon, where brand differentiation is limited largely to price. As such, hotels, airlines, and other similar industries have to compete on multiple fronts—cut prices while advertising, innovating service, and introducing new products—to even consider sustained profitability.

It's like trying to run your household after losing some of your salary while keeping up with the neighbors. The economics just don't make a lot of sense.

There are examples where rivalry works to ensure economic moats. Coke and Pepsi have both managed to sustain profitability without depending solely on price. While they are rivals, they offer very similar product lines, though they breed a sense of loyalty among consumers. Coca-Cola is also the clear industry leader. Unlike the airlines, where many carriers were relative equals, forcing them all to compete against one another for primacy, Coca-Cola's market share leaves it firmly in control. Consumers don't have a lot of power in the pricing structure for soft drinks, but they tend to have preferences in terms of the products they enjoy. Consumer preference is based here on taste, while in the airline industry, it is based almost completely on price.

Consumer control over pricing is the second, and often less considered, of Porter's Five Forces. Consumers are competing for industry pricing—often as much as or more than companies within the industry themselves. If consumers can shop around for comparable products or services without sacrificing end goals too much, then overall industry profitability becomes price reliant. Take, for example, the American auto industry. Apart from the truly brand loyal, most consumers will happily look at similar cars—sedans, vans, SUVs, trucks, and so on—from multiple makers and "comparison shop." As a buyer, it's just good business. Look at comparable models from multiple manufacturers and the same model from multiple dealers, all in the pursuit of the "best deal."

Like the airlines, consumers exert control through options, with little end-product differentiation, and companies have to "buy" consumers by sacrificing profitability. The industries hurt the worst (publicly anyway) in the last recession were the ones most affected by consumer choice. The airlines, cruise lines, and car manufacturers all suffered from Internet price shopping made easy. The digital revolution, while opening the world to a universe of possibility, also made it hard for once seemingly solid industries to cope, leaving companies vulnerable to price pressures exerted by empowered consumers presented with a raft of options that would satisfy an end goal with little deviation and variation.

Then there's always the competition that comes from newcomers. The ubiquity of Coke and Pepsi—solid numbers one and two in the market—also makes it difficult for new competitors to arise, which is the third of Porter's five forces: aspiring industry entrants.

Barriers to Entry

Barriers to entry for new entrants into an industry are indicators that a particular company has long-term profitability potential. When I talk to friends and clients about barriers to entry, I like to use the example of a gravel company. If I were to start a company today, in any industry, gravel would not make the list of potential industries. Why? Because it is an industry that favors the incumbent in almost every way. For one thing, it's highly regulated. Getting the necessary permits and approvals involves years of bureaucratic hassles, expensive studies, and impact reports—all after you find a plot of land suitable for excavation. Once you gain the necessary improvements, gravel mining requires major capital investments just to begin to break rocks, and should you survive the mire of oversight and secure your equipment, find the skilled labor necessary to operate it, and begin creating product, you've still got the issue of breaking into a relatively small, tight-knit market dominated by multigenerational or otherwise established leaders. And you've got to do all this before ever seeing a dime. In that same amount of time and for considerably less money, I could have opened a coffee shop in every strip mall in the greater metropolitan area.

Gravel mining has durable competitive advantages associated with these barriers to entry, and it's why sometimes the companies that pass this first filter in the 52-Week Low formula are not ones you've ever heard of. Competitive advantage does not manifest itself in popularity or pop cultural awareness, but in the forces at work that limit the possibility of an upstart company quickly growing to steal market share and change the nature of competition. Nor does it mean that the companies that enjoy profit protection in the form of barriers to entry are small. Supply-side economies of scale often serve as barrier enough. The big companies that produce large volumes of their products can get the raw materials needed to make those products at a much more competitive rate. They get a break, in no uncertain terms, for buying in bulk. This makes it hard for new entrants into the market to compete; they simply can't get the same deals from their suppliers that the larger firms can.

Pat Dorsey provides a lot of examples and insights into identifying moats in his book *The Little Book that Builds Wealth.*

One, specifically, that Dorsey cites is the kinds of companies people don't want around them:

> My favorite example of this is what I call the NIMBY ("not in my backyard") companies, such as waste haulers and aggregate producers. After all, who wants a landfill or stone quarry located in their neighborhood? Almost no one, which means that existing landfills and stone quarries are extremely valuable. As such, getting new ones approved is close to impossible.
>
> Trash and gravel may not sound exciting, but the moat created by scores of mini-approvals is very durable. After all, companies like trash haulers and aggregate firms rely on hundreds of municipal-level approvals that are unlikely to disappear overnight en masse. What really makes these locally approved landfills and quarries so valuable for companies like Waste Management and Vulcan Materials is that waste and gravel are inherently local businesses. You can't profitably dump trash hundreds of miles from where it is collected, and you can't truck aggregates much farther than 40 or 50 miles from a quarry without pricing yourself out of the market. (Trash is heavy, and gravel is even heavier.) So, local approvals for landfills and quarries create scores of mini-moats in these industries.[3]

On the consumer demand side, incumbents enjoying high barriers to entry also benefit from a wide degree of usage.

Network Effect

Network effect, as discussed in Dorsey's book, relates to companies like Visa—most customers have a Visa credit card,

---

[3] Pat Dorsey, *The Little Book that Builds Wealth: The Knockout Formula for Finding Great Investments* (Hoboken, NJ: Wiley, 2008).

which forces merchants to accept Visa and that network builds on and on.

Another example and one that not many investors are familiar with is Ritchie Brothers. The world's largest industrial auctioneer has maintained stable operating margins over the last 10 years due to its Network Effect. It is an auctioneer that is trusted by both buyers and sellers.

Here is what Morningstar had to say about Ritchie Brothers' Moat in September 2013:

> We think Ritchie Bros.' ability to create a vast network of global auction sites helps the firm garner a wide economic moat. This larger network results in a greater liquidity pool of buyers and sellers than its competitors can offer, so Ritchie Bros. auctions should deliver the best market-clearing price. As the number of buyers and sellers swells, a cycle occurs that continues to attract more participants to the firm's auction, making it nearly impossible for a competitor to permeate Ritchie Bros.' fortress. Ritchie Bros. is already the world's largest industrial auctioneer—10 times bigger than its nearest competitor—and it sells more used equipment to on-site and online bidders than any other company, including original-equipment manufacturers. This impervious auction site network has helped the firm generate average returns on invested capital of 16 percent during the past decade, well in excess of our estimated cost of capital. We contend that it would take a substantial amount of time for a competitor to create a network of a similar stature, and we think Ritchie Bros. deserves a wide economic moat.[4]

If a company produces a specialized product or service, for example, payment tools or industrial auctions, it is

---

[4]Morningstar, "Ritchie Bros. Auctioneers, Inc.," http://analysisreport.morningstar .com/stock/archive?t=RBA&region=USA&&culture=en-US&docId=610490.

protected by its own offering. It specializes in something for which there is great demand and becomes associated with that specialized product to the point where it becomes easier for that company to add customers than it would be for a new company to earn them. In order for a new entrant to build a customer base, it will be forced to sell at a discount. Given that the entrenched company can dig deeper into profit margins thanks to its supply-side economies of scale and still make a profit, the price war rarely works out for the new guy on the block.

Switching Cost

Do you ever wonder why banks give away their Web bill-pay service and direct deposit for free? It is a hidden profitable hook for banks to give this service away, because once you have taken the time to have all of your bills set up to be paid out of your checking account, what is the likelihood that you will ever switch? A better question: how long have you used your bank that has the Web bill-pay service? I'll bet for a while, and it will probably be for a while longer. It would be too much of a pain to switch.

There are other businesses with very high switching costs. Payroll providers, as an example, benefit greatly from high switching costs. Here's Morningstar's analysis on the competitive landscape—or lack thereof—experienced by both ADP and Paychex:

> ADP's scale, high customer switching costs, and respected brand image provide the firm with strong competitive advantages. The firm assists business customers with all aspects of their payroll processing functions, from paying client employees and tax authorities to wage garnishments. The firm has approximately a 30 percent share (based on revenue) of the payroll outsourcing market with more than 600,000 clients. It can leverage its size and minimal

capital requirements into substantial scale advantages. Long-term contracts and the difficulty inherent in switching outsourced human resources processes to another provider allow ADP to lock clients into its services. Average client retention is estimated to be more than 10 years, and this stickiness allows ADP to raise prices annually with very little resistance. Its major competitor, Paychex, has approximately 11 percent market share, effectively creating a duopoly that has allowed both firms to enjoy hefty margins. Even though they compete with similar services, they have left each other alone for the most part in order to exploit different segments of the payroll outsourcing market, with ADP focusing on larger customers. As such, profit-draining competition has been avoided, with both firms reaping the rewards.[5]

But let's say somehow a new company stands itself up and manages to get products manufactured. There's still the consideration of switching costs—the costs for a consumer (or customer) to leave their current supplier and go with a new one. If I'm a manufacturer, will switching to a new vendor require retooling? Training for my employees? A change or break in my own process? These are the hidden costs of bouncing from supplier to supplier. Companies in industries with high switching costs insulate themselves from new entrant competition. Durable competitive advantages rely on these kinds of costs to be sustained. Industries without them—like hotels, airlines, most clothiers, and coffee shops, where the cost for consumers to switch brands or suppliers, if one exists, is low—remain vulnerable to upstart competition.

[5] Morningstar, "Automatic Data Processing," http://analysisreport.morningstar.com/stock/research?t=ADP&region=usa&culture=en-US&ownerCountry=USA.

Powerful Suppliers

While economies of scale with suppliers can serve to insulate bigger, more established incumbents from new entries into a market, powerful suppliers can influence profitability in the same way. Suppliers are not just other companies providing parts or material for the manufacture of goods, but labor—particularly organized or otherwise regulated labor—can play a major role in determining a company's profitability. Look at the steel industry for a perfect example of this. The U.S. steel industry long thrived on quality and the relative protection of geographic isolation. U.S. steel makers were making better steel than was available elsewhere, and as the industry grew, so, too, did the demands of the labor involved. This is not a knock on unions—after all, they offer protection for workers who might otherwise be exploited or mistreated—but organized labor created higher innate supplier costs for U.S. steel manufacturers. Once quality improved in foreign manufacturing, where fixed labor costs were much lower, and transportation improvements made it easier for end users of steel to import from these foreign manufacturers at a lesser cost than buying domestically, the writing was on the wall. Say what you will about the politics involved, but from an economic perspective, it was an implosion waiting to happen.

Identifying companies in industries that have a low risk of being subject to powerful suppliers helps to ensure sound economics and long-term profitability. But the final of Porter's five forces is crucial to ensuring profit potential, and it begins by asking a simple question–are there readily available substitutes that will work just as well and create a threat to sustainable profits?

Substitute Offerings

In his paper, Porter identifies a few such ready-made substitutes that may or may not be obvious.

"A substitute performs the same or a similar function as an industry's product by a different means," he writes. "Video-conferencing is a substitute for travel. Plastic is a substitute for aluminum. E-mail is a substitute for express mail."[6]

Substitutes are often the unseen or unconsidered rivals that pose a major threat, particularly in a time when digital communication is changing the way we live, on-demand manufacturing is changing the way we make things, and outsourcing is becoming a way we do business. Even where we live can create unforeseen substitution threats.

Not a lot of camera manufacturers saw the threat to their market share coming from smartphones and other multiuse devices.

Identifying substitution threats requires critical thinking beyond the balance sheet, industry reporting, and other traditional data that inform strategy. It requires thinking practically. If I no longer have to carry a camera but can take pictures with my phone, what are the consequential substitutions that arise from changes in the way I capture images? This kind of analysis, in addition to identifying threats, can also reveal opportunities.

In the early 2000s, when the record companies were fighting for the remains of profits left after the file-sharing revolution ravaged their stronghold on music sales, it was a company from a seemingly unrelated industry that revolutionized the way we buy, consume, and archive music. Apple's creation of iTunes was not simply a way for you and I to get copies of the music we love, but an end-to-end solution for the way we consume it. Our relationship with music, which for a century had been defined by the acquisition, storage, and playing of records, tapes, eight-tracks, and compact discs (CDs), was transformed when we could put a thousand

---

[6]Porter, 2008.

songs in our pocket. And no longer did we need to buy whole albums when all we wanted was a single song. We were able to simply buy that song.

What, for the next generations, will seem so intuitive and the only way they know how to buy music, represents a substitution in our lives. When it became just as easy to buy plane tickets from third-party travel sites as it was to go through a travel agent, the writing was on the wall. When it became easier to do so, the substitution was complete, and the travel agency as we had known it for a half-century became a thing of the past. In the 1960s, our culture saw the advent of the shopping mall. The 1980s was about the rise of the mega-store. But Jeff Bezos saw an opportunity for substitution that allowed people to buy nearly anything they wanted without leaving the comfort of their homes, and the introduction of overnight shipping and the Prime account from Amazon that makes it free for frequent customers means the days of paving over farmland to put up a shopping center are limited.

Understanding the power of substitution and thinking critically about the threat it poses to a particular company or industry is crucial to understanding the long-term prospects for profit.

What to Look For

While it's always dangerous to offer specific investment recommendations in a book—since months, perhaps even years, have passed between the moment I put these words on paper in the fall of 2013 and the time you are reading it—I find it's often best to use specific examples to illustrate a larger point.

Porter and other investment strategists, like Bruce Greenwald and Judd Kahn, do a good job of illustrating the forces at work in either creating or eroding economic moats and durable competitive advantages.

Competition comes in many forms:

- Rivalry among established players
- Powerful suppliers
- Empowered consumers
- New entrants
- Readily available alternatives

But what are some real-world examples of those forces at work? How, when you sit down with your adviser, do you begin to identify these factors? The answer to that is simple: you do your homework.

Western Union (WU)

This chapter began with a discussion of Western Union. What many Americans, particularly middle- and upper-class Americans, might view as an antiquated business model and service in our twenty-first-century, technology-driven time, is, to a lot of the rest of the world, still the best option.

Morningstar analyst Brett Horn specifically cites the network effect at work as a durable, though incremental, advantage for Western Union. Around the world, more than 500,000 agents make up a vast and growing network of locations able to send and receive money efficiently. With every new agent that signs on, the network grows. As the network continues to grow, its authority and attractiveness to new agents grows. In this way, it becomes self-fulfilling. There's a sense of "everyone else is doing it, so maybe I should, too, if I want to get into the money transfer business."

But, you might ask, can't we do this with the Internet? Or our cell phones? Can't we just open an app and send money to someone? The answer is both yes and no. There are alternative transfer methods out there. PayPal is a growing one, but there's a specific problem to a completely Web-based solution: you have to have the infrastructure to access the Web.

"In our opinion, a wide-scale industry switch to alternative methods would require a dramatic improvement in electronic payment infrastructures on a global scale," Horn writes, "a change that is likely to take a very long time."[7]

In other words, Western Union's moat is strengthened by a disproportionate and globally inconsistent technology development progress. You may live in a country with wireless cities and smartphones in every pocket, but if you are sending money to someone in a less developed country, they don't have the technological infrastructure to receive it. Late adoption to new methods, technologies, and platforms by the recipient countries means Western Union can continue to grow with its existing method while developing infrastructure to adapt to new methods in the future.

Visa (V)

Another company in a similar industry that enjoys a similar moat related to the network effect is Visa. While we commonly look in our wallets, see the Visa logo, and associate it with credit cards, the fact is that Visa is not a bank, but a payment logistics company.

Jim Sinegal, a Morningstar analyst, identifies two major factors contributing to Visa's competitive advantage that should protect the company for years and decades to come: acceptance and trust.

Like Western Union, Visa gains from the fact that it takes two to tango in the payment logistics industry. As cash continues to fall by the wayside as a preferred payment method in developed countries, companies like Visa will continue to grow. And growing industries tend to attract new entrants, but Visa's incumbency is a major advantage. It's widely accepted as a payment method by merchants, which is

---

[7]Morningstar, "Western Union," http://analysisreport.morningstar.com/stock/archive?t=WU&region=USA&&culture=en-US&docId=601632.

attractive to consumers—acceptance of a method is essential to using that method—and the more attractive it is to consumers, the more likely a merchant is to use it. This symbiotic relationship is key to Visa's long-term growth and has been for decades.

Also key to growth is the trust associated with a payment logistics company you know. Trust is the benefit of ubiquity and serves as a barrier of entry to newcomers. People trust Visa. Merchants trust Visa. And Visa has invested billions into the intangible asset of trust, according to Sinegal. That investment has been in advertising, security, and efficiency, all of which serve merchants and consumers well and help to keep and grow their trust, which, in turn, bolsters usage, which bolsters acceptance, which creates competitive advantages that result in long-term profitability.

Campbell's (CPB)

Visa and Western Union have competitive advantages based on a lack of readily available alternatives, but what about a company for which the moat is built on supplier and consumer forces?

Campbell's owns the U.S. "wet" soup market. Analyst Erin Lash, CFA, analyst for Morningstar, says the company's stronghold is roughly 60 percent of the market. Impressive, to say the least. And while consumers do have some choice when it comes to soup, Campbell's established ubiquity and expansive global distribution network set it up for sustained success. It's going to be tough for new entrants to come into the soup industry and make a dent in Campbell's. Not only do they dominate shelf space, the company operates with "unrivaled economies of scale," when it comes to suppliers, according to Lash.

From the vegetables and protein to cans and labels, Campbell's size means it has a controlling price position with suppliers. There may be other soups on the shelf, but unfamiliar offerings from less familiar brands at what are almost certain to be higher prices limits the pool of consumers who may make a switch. The name you know, the soup you like, at a price you can appreciate—that's the Campbell's competitive advantage story in a nutshell.

Fastenal (FAST)

Fastenal is a leader in industrial and commercial fastener manufacturing, distribution, and sales, and its competitive advantage is a case study in creating moats based on operational efficiency, ubiquity, diversification of offerings, and the benefits of being entrenched.

Morningstar analyst Basili Alukos, CPA, CFA, points out two problems that, on paper, may mean trouble for Fastenal but is quick to show how the company is positioned to protect itself from those threats. First, industrial and commercial fasteners are low-cost and generally don't have innately high switching costs for consumers. Alternative options are readily available, which leads to the second problem: a growing industry with low (or nonexistent) switching costs is bound to attract new entrants.

So how does Fastenal maintain a competitive advantage in a growing industry composed of low-cost, easy-to-replace products? By beating competitors to the punch.

Fastenal has a product catalog of more than 592,000 products and massive scale advantages over upstart competition. It has a vast geographical presence, with more than 2,700 stores and 14 distribution centers, and a fulfillment system powered by 100,000 daily pickups and 80 percent delivery of products before 8 A.M. Manufacturers don't want to have to keep warehouses full of fasteners. It's wasted space. So this just-in-time delivery method reduces inventory costs and a whole world of hassle. It's cheaper, too. Fastenal claims that its distribution method is 10 times cheaper than other companies that use third-party distribution methods.

Fasteners, because of their low costs and the nature of their usage, are a low-consideration purchase for supply managers, and Fastenal has created a moat by making the decision easy, saving money on distribution, and offering more products than anyone else without forcing customers to carry big inventories of their products. It is, essentially, a one-stop shop—and a profitable one at that.

Since 1997, Fastenal has maintained an average gross margin of 51 percent. This means that even if a competitor were to find their way into the market, Fastenal (through efficiencies and economies of scale) has the ability to engage in a price war. From the looks of it, however, that won't be necessary. The question will remain whether Fastenal can continue to expand offerings while keeping prices down, but unlike competitors, they are in a position to innovate around those considerations.

Fastenal shows that while alternative products are available and consumers have some power through low switching costs, boosting other forces of competitive advantage can compensate for those threats.

Waters (WAT)

While the other companies I've discussed in this chapter are probably familiar to most people, it's important to look at companies you may know little to nothing about in order to understand that popular awareness is not always a factor in competitive advantage.

Unless you work in the pharmaceutical industry, you may never have heard of Waters. It is a company that specializes in manufacturing and design of mass spectrometry and liquid chromatography equipment for pharmaceutical and governmental applications and one that enjoys a "wide moat," according to Morningstar's Alex Morozov, CFA, because of high switching costs, lack of available alternatives, an "unmatched" technological engine, and a long upgrade cycle that limits consumer alternatives.

When a researcher begins work on a new drug using Waters's mass spectrometry or liquid chromatography equipment, it's highly likely they will continue using the equipment through the development process, writes Morozov. And that process can take years to complete. Switching costs for customers are incredibly high in this regard and serve to protect Waters's advantage.

"Instruments become ingrained in the drug-manufacturing process," Morozov writes.[8]

Customers are also slow to upgrade or change, a cycle that can take five years or more to complete. While technological advantages are usually fleeting, Waters holds its position on the cutting edge, and the long upgrade cycle serves to support it.

Summing It Up

These are just a few examples of companies that would pass the first of the 52-Week Low's five filters.

While many investment strategies take different approaches to identifying companies with earnings potential, the 52-Week Low formula starts with economics, specifically, the economics of competition. Good companies will go through bad times, making them ripe for the picking for savvy investors, provided the hard times are not the cause of bad economics but rather short-term headwinds that create an undervaluation or opportunity.

Look for companies and industries with good economics and you'll be ready to move onto the next of the five filters in the 52-Week Low formula.

---

[8]Morningstar, "Waters Corporation," http://analysisreport.morningstar.com/stock/archive?t=WAT&region=USA&&&culture=en-US&docId=591357.

Case Study: The Story of a Dollar: 1980–2012

The value of the dollar has changed significantly over the years. But, for investors, the value of a dollar invested is an indication of how well an investment strategy works to compound earnings over time. While past performance is not a guarantee of future results, doing these sorts of regression studies helps to illustrate unexpected strengths. In this case study, we will see how the 52-Week Low helps to participate less in market bubbles while recovering sooner following economic downturns.

But, first, let's look at the past 30 years. Investment research firm Empiritrage conducted back testing of how the 52-Week Low formula performed against the Standard & Poor's (S&P) 500 between 1980 and 2012. We'll look at a couple of specific time periods a little later in this chapter, but first some data.

Empiritrage's independent testing examined the journey of a single dollar invested in both the 52-Week Low formula and the S&P 500. Both investments were equally valuable in 1980: $1. But what happens over the next 32 years reveals why the 52-Week Low approach is so valuable not only in the long run but also during market meltdowns.

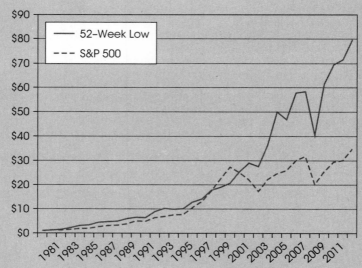

Figure 3.1   A Dollar Invested in the 52-Week Low Formula versus S&P 500

By 2012, that single dollar invested in the S&P 500 was worth $34.87, while the dollar invested in the 52-Week Low formula was worth $79.69—more than twice that of the market investment.

The question then becomes: why?

At no point in the 32-year test did the $1 worth of principal become worth less than $1, and for the first 15 years, growth followed similar trajectories in the 52-Week Low and the S&P. Then, in 1995, the S&P began to outpace the 52-Week Low. In fact, between 1995 and 1999, the S&P rose sharply, while the 52-Week Low continued at a pace similar to the previous decade.

This was the tech bubble (Figure 3.2), those halcyon days when it seemed every 20-year-old with an idea in Silicon Valley was getting $10 million in angel funding, and for a few years, it seemed the sky was the limit. By 1995, that original dollar invested in the S&P was worth $10.58, and over the next five years, it nearly tripled to $27.32. Everyone was making money, so long as they were invested in tech stocks.

But the 52-Week Low formula did not include any dot-com stocks or companies with zero or negative free cash flow, and, consequently, for this time period, it and other value strategies, like those of Warren Buffett, underperformed against the market.

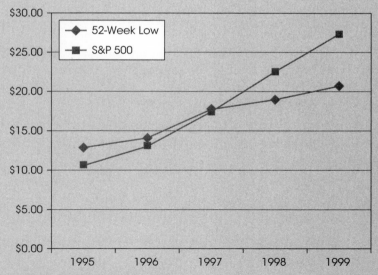

Figure 3.2   The Tech Bubble

(*continued*)

(*continued*)

One of the core tenets of the 52-Week Low strategy is to identify valuable companies during periods when they are undervalued. The first of the five filters that make up the strategy identifies companies with curable competitive advantages in industries with strong economics. Many pockets within the tech industry—which during this time produced such iconic companies as Pets.com—did not have strong economics. Competitive advantages were fleeting. The moat a company in some of these subset industries had during this time was threatened by the next programmer in the next garage down the street.

If for no other reason, this flimsy economic model and a lack of durable competitive advantages meant the 52-Week Low stayed out of the dot-com bubble as it was growing—seemingly without an end in sight.

But we all know what happened next. In fact, we should have seen it coming. Legendary investor Sir John Templeton once said that the four most dangerous words in investing are: "It's different this time." And with good reason. The dot-com bubble seemed new and exciting. Our world was changing, getting smaller and more connected. We were seduced by the newness of the technology, the novelty of the Internet. The world was changing. Humanity was changing. The sky seemed to be the limit.

In August 2000, *Fortune* magazine published an article titled "10 Stocks to Last the Decade." *

A decade later, CBS published an article titled "How Not to Create a Fortune,"[†] which followed up on those "10 Stocks to Last the Decade." How do you think they did?

Following are the total returns of *Fortune*'s picks, as well as the total return of some simple benchmarks for the period from January 2000 through December 2009.

Genentech (DNA): 182.4 percent (Note: Genentech was acquired for cash in 2009.)
Oracle (ORCL): −11.8 percent
Charles Schwab (SCHW): −16.8 percent

---

* David Rynecki, "10 Stocks to Last the Decade," *Fortune*, August 14, 2000, http://money.cnn .com/magazines/fortune/fortune_archive/2000/08/14/285599/index.htm.
† Larry Swedroe, "How Not to Create a Fortune," *CBS Moneywatch*, July 7, 2010, www. cbsnews.com/news/how-not-to-create-a-fortune.

Univision: −30.7 percent (Note: Univision was sold to a private
    company in 2006.)
Morgan Stanley (MS): −39.6 percent
Viacom (Class B) (VIA-B): −61.2 percent (Note: In 2006, Viacom
    was split into two companies, Viacom and CBS. The return
    reflects an investment in both companies from that point.)
Broadcom (BRCM): −65.3 percent
Nokia (NOK): −67.1 percent
Nortel: −100 percent
Enron: −100 percent

All but one of the "stocks for the decade" not only lost money, but
also underperformed benchmarks.

Russell 2000 Value Index: 121.3 percent
Russell 2000 Index: −41.2 percent
CRSP Deciles 1–10 Index: −3.2 percent
S&P 500 Index: −9.1 percent

Only one single stock outperformed an appropriate benchmark
(Genetch), two went bankrupt, and the average pick lost 31 percent.
The lesson is that valuation matters.
And, even by the year 2000, we should have known much better.
Was this euphoric time and bubble burst unique by historical
standards, or has this irrational behavior taken place throughout the
centuries? In the mid-1630s a craze swept Holland that changed the
course of economic history. Tulips, the beautiful flowers we give to our
moms every Mother's Day, became the seventeenth-century equiva-
lent of the dot-com bubble. According to *The Economist*,[‡] tulip prices
increased by as much as 2,000 percent in just three months.

Tulpenwoede (tulip madness) resulted in big increases in tulip
prices. At the beginning of 1637, some tulip contracts reached a level
about 20 times the level of three months earlier. A particularly rare
tulip, Semper Augustus, was priced at around 1,000 guilders in the
1620s. But just before the crash, it was valued at 5,500 guilders per
bulb—roughly the cost of a luxurious house in Amsterdam. Prices
collapsed in February 1637, and more than a few investors were left
bankrupt.

[‡] "Was Tulipmania Irrational?" *The Economist, (Free Exchange* blog), October 4, 2013, www
.economist.com/blogs/freeexchange/2013/10/economic-history.

(continued)

(continued)

So what happened? Did tulips become more valuable? Did they become more useful? Did tulips all of a sudden cure disease or give people superhuman strength or mental acumen?

No.

Economic historians debate the central causes of tulip mania. Some, like nineteenth-century Scottish writer Charles Mackay, blame it on irrationality. Others, like Peter Garber, blame uncertainty about life expectancy: He reckons that an outbreak of bubonic plague in Amsterdam made people less risk averse. Dutch city dwellers knew that each day could be their last, so they did not mind indulging in a little speculation. And because gambling was illegal, contracts were unenforceable. If traders misjudged the market, they could just run off without paying.

There are arguments that the cause of the phenomenon was a "rational response to changes in financial regulation" and others for speculation. The mania was blamed on the general public's chasing profits, not on serious tulip financiers, who seemed to avoid the frenzy.

Much the same way that Dutch hopefuls plunked down larger and larger sums for the possibility of getting rich off tulip mania, so, too, did amateurs, day traders, and those seeking quick profits over sustained value chased the dot-coms. Investors were caring less and

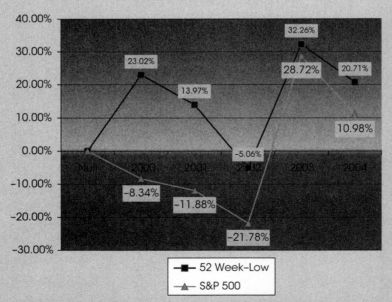

Figure 3.3   52-Week Low Performance versus S&P 500 Performance during Dot-Com Bust

less about corporate earnings and valuations and were, instead, wanting more and more only of companies where there was a high degree of enthusiasm.

Tulip prices tumbled—not rocketed—down in mid-1637, leaving many broken and holding the bag for having invested in a fad instead of value. The economy that had propelled growth at unprecedented levels crashed and crashed hard.

American humorist and writer Mark Twain once said that "history doesn't repeat itself, but it does rhyme." And the rhyme of the tulip debacle was the dot-com bust.

After five years of above-average growth, the S&P 500 began to fall. The value of that dollar invested staggered (Table 3.1), even as the dollar invested in the 52-Week Low formula continued to rise when stock valuations and rationality began to matter again (Figures 3.3 and 3.5).

Table 3.1 shows the 10-year performance leading up to the dot-com bubble and what happened following the burst.

Table 3.1 52-Week Low Performance, 1995–2004

Year	Performance	52-Week Low	$Value	S&P 500	$Value
			$1.00		$1.00
1995	Underperform	27.40%	$1.27	37.64%	$1.38
1996	Underperform	9.53%	$1.40	23.23%	$1.70
1997	Underperform	25.74%	$1.75	33.60%	$2.27
1998	Underperform	7.01%	$1.88	29.32%	$2.93
1999	Underperform	9.20%	$2.05	21.35%	$3.56
2000	Outperform	23.02%	$2.52	−8.34%	$3.26
2001	Outperform	13.97%	$2.87	−11.88%	$2.87
2002	Outperform	−5.06%	$2.73	−21.78%	$2.25
2003	Outperform	32.26%	$3.61	28.72%	$2.89
2004	Outperform	20.71%	$4.36	10.98%	$3.21

The volatility and return over this cycle were:

	52-Week Low	S&P 500
Standard Deviation	11.43%	21.06%
Geometric Mean	15.86%	12.37%
Correlation Coefficient: 0.50145		

(continued)

(*continued*)

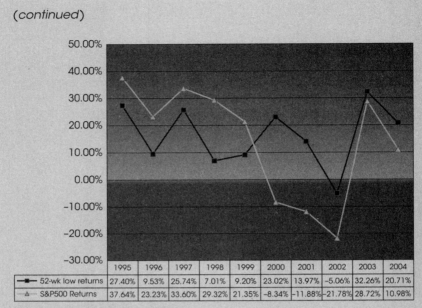

	1995	1996	1997	1998	1999	2000	2001	2002	2003	2004
52-wk low returns	27.40%	9.53%	25.74%	7.01%	9.20%	23.02%	13.97%	-5.06%	32.26%	20.71%
S&P500 Returns	37.64%	23.23%	33.60%	29.32%	21.35%	-8.34%	-11.88%	-21.78%	28.72%	10.98%

Figure 3.4   Comparing Returns

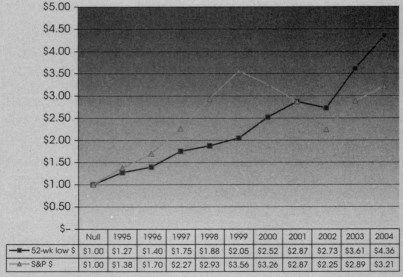

	Null	1995	1996	1997	1998	1999	2000	2001	2002	2003	2004
52-wk low $	$1.00	$1.27	$1.40	$1.75	$1.88	$2.05	$2.52	$2.87	$2.73	$3.61	$4.36
S&P $	$1.00	$1.38	$1.70	$2.27	$2.93	$3.56	$3.26	$2.87	$2.25	$2.89	$3.21

Figure 3.5   Tracking a Dollar

In 2000, the dot-com bubble had burst and the market began to fall. In 2001, following the attacks of September 11, the market was not in a position to weather the crisis. It wasn't until 2003 that the S&P 500 began a slow growth trend.

Meanwhile, value investors and the 52-Week Low weathered the dot-com bust by simply avoiding it. It hardly lost in the period between January 2000, and when the economy began to pick back up in 2003. Then, it went on to set a new, blistering (by comparison) pace for growth.

The extra $1.50 in value that the S&P 500 dollar gained during the dot-com bubble, as shown in Figure 3.5, was obliterated by the growth of the 52-Week Low dollar following the bust. In fact, by the end of 2004, the value of the 52-Week Low dollar ($4.36) was substantially more (35 percent) than that of the S&P 500 dollar value ($3.21), as shown in Figure 3.5.

Did we learn anything from the dot-com bubble? Apparently not much. Real estate, which we'll look at a little closer in another case study, created a bubble that nearly crippled the U.S. economy just four years later. Did that teach us? Well, I'm not sure.

On September 21, 2012, Apple closed above $700, and most analysts thought it had only one way to go. One analyst even put a 12-month target at $1,000 per share. At the time, I remember hearing interviews with people who were putting their entire 401(k) into the company. And why not? It seems liked everyone is making money from the pride of Cupertino (Apple).

But history is bound to rhyme once again. Will Apple mania be studied a century from now the way tulip mania has been studied for centuries? I think so. Any time craze leads to investment, we need to be skeptical. Any time enthusiasm trumps logic and a system, we are allowing our emotions to get the better of us.

We have to be careful when we start believing it's different this time.

Howard Marks, in his book *The Most Important Thing: Uncommon Sense for the Thoughtful Investor,* stated that skepticism and pessimism aren't synonymous. Skepticism calls for pessimism when optimism is excessive. But it also calls for optimism when pessimism is excessive.

Value-investing strategies, like the 52-Week Low, help to eliminate hope and enthusiasm from the consideration set when making investment decisions. And as history continues to rhyme in the future, we have good reason to believe that skipping out on a craze in favor of real value pays off.

CHAPTER 4

Five Common Mistakes Investors Make

*J*acobian Inverse: *What are some common mistakes that could help me destroy my principal with a high probability? I would rather follow my instincts than pause and contemplate a better way to think and behave.*

Pausing and raising your awareness of how we instinctively and often inaccurately behave should help you better grow your principal rather than destroy your principal.

I've been working in finance for more than 15 years. In that time, I've worked with hundreds of clients, dozens of investment managers and Wall Street analysts, and while the world of investments is a constantly changing, ever-evolving one, there are certain mistakes or pitfalls that I've seen consistently over time. These mistakes are not limited to bad investments. In fact, bad investments tend to be the results of mistakes, not the mistakes themselves. The mistakes I've seen over the years happen long before a trade is executed. They are mental mistakes, psychological mistakes, and, for the most part, they are completely avoidable. There are more than five, but these are the most common ones I've seen and the ones most likely to lead to investor dissatisfaction, disappointment, and poor results.

Mistake 1: Trusting Your Emotions Instead of Engaging the Mind

I'm a fairly emotional guy. I understand the power of feelings, but when it comes to investments, emotions need to take a backseat to logic, rules, and discipline. The most common emotion in money management is fear—fear of losing, fear of missing out, fear of the unknown. Following fear is unfounded optimism. Buying a hot stock—one that's been on the rise and is making people money—is a fool's errand. Competition is high, driving the price higher, and overvaluing a company will eventually lead to loss. The same goes for good companies that are on the decline. Holding on to a stock with the hopes that it will rebound makes no sense on paper. It's only in the murky recesses of our brains and hearts that we can make sense of that. Don't buy out of hope or fear; don't invest with your heart on your sleeve. Instead, make sound decisions based on clear rules and principles— like the 52-Week Low formula—and take emotion out of the equation.

Benjamin Graham, the "Father of Value Investing," put it this way: "Individuals who cannot master their emotions are ill-suited to profit from the investment process."

In a 2009 presentation titled "Behavioral Pitfalls in Periods of Economic Uncertainty," UBS Wealth Management Research identified common emotions that correspond to market performance. This presentation was distributed at the bottom of the last bear market. This presentation was not only quite timely but quite accurate (see Figures 4.1 and 4.2).

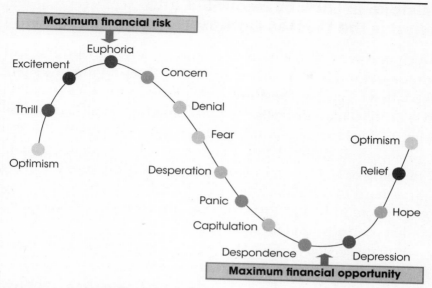

Figure 4.1   The Emotional Market

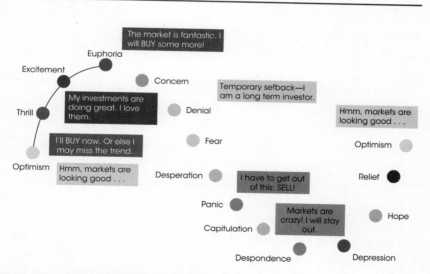

Figure 4.2   The Emotional Market, Part II
Source: UBS Wealth Management.

Mistake 2: Lack of Discipline and What is the Ulysses Contract?

Discipline is hard. It's hard to get up on a rainy morning and go for a run. It's hard to say no to that slice of grandma's pie. But when it comes to investing, discipline has to be a way of life. You need to have discipline to make good up-front decisions— what to buy and why—and, perhaps most important, the discipline to sell. When I buy a company, I know the exact date I'm going to sell it, regardless of how well it's doing. It can be just as hard to sell a stock that's performing well as it is to drag yourself out of bed for that run, but not having a sell discipline could eventually (and inevitably) cost you.

Process is vital in life. Having a regimen, a process, helps you maintain your health. What's a diet if not a process, a checklist to follow? Having established processes removes some of the need to make decisions that can be influenced by emotion, timidity, or other external factors.

Atul Gawande is a journalist and surgeon widely known as an expert on reducing error, improving efficiency, and improving safety in modern surgery. He lives by a checklist as a means of ensuring process and describes its value this way:

> It is common to misconceive how checklists function in complex lines of work. They are not comprehensive how-to guides, whether for building a skyscraper or getting a plane out of trouble. They are quick and simple tools aimed to buttress the skills of expert professionals. And by remaining swift and usable and resolutely modest, they are saving thousands upon thousands of lives.[1]

Many of you can probably think back to junior high school and remember reading Homer's *Odyssey*, the epic tale of

---

[1]From Atul Gawande, *The Checklist Manifesto: How to Get Things Right* (New York: Metropolitan Books, 2009).

Ulysses and his band of men struggling against morality and nature in a tough and unforgiving world. I'm not one of them. To be honest, I don't remember having ever heard of the book until I was an adult, but one part of the story has stuck with me and it's the part dealing with the pact Ulysses makes with his men as they sail near the dangerous Sirens.

Ulysses knows he will be tempted by the intoxicating song of the Sirens. He knows how hard it will be to resist and that not resisting will surely cost him his life. Some people might believe they have willpower enough to resist temptation, but Ulysses was smarter than that. He knew he would not be able to resist on his own, so he asks his men to tie him to the mast of his ship and not release him, no matter how hard he struggles, how much he begs, no matter the promises or threats he makes to let him go.

Ulysses understood human frailty the same way Gawande does. He understood that, left to our own devices and without systems in place, we are bound to make decisions that produce terrible effects.

Investors have adopted the insights of Ulysses and Gawande in the form of a Ulysses contract. Essentially, it's an agreement between an investor and his or her advisor of the course they will take in the event of a catastrophe or euphoria. They look at the road ahead, plan for contingency, and agree to what will be done. They pre-commit to a strategy and tie their investments to the mast.

This means not just committing to a course of action when things are good—not chasing after boom stocks and crowds, for example—but agreeing to a disciplined approach to ride out tough times—not agreeing to a six-month reassessment and then freaking out and selling two months in, for example.

Having rules and means of following them will bolster, if not outright ensure, a disciplined approach to investing that can help avoid common pitfalls.

Mistake 3: Apathy the Halo Effect

It's always been puzzling to me to see clients accept their adviser's advice without asking some really hard questions. I've seen it time and again. Clients put their money where their advisers tell them to without asking why, without challenging the logic or the strategy. They fill out some forms about goals and budgets and blithely go where their advisers tell them to go.

I want my clients to challenge me. It forces me to work harder, to ask critical questions before they come up, to challenge my own assumptions, and to strengthen my planning. I like it when a new client challenges my thinking—particularly on the 52-Week Low formula—because it gives me an opportunity to explain it further to them, to make them understand. If I can do that, then I know I've done my job. This isn't to say that investors should be watching their portfolio performance every minute of every day; after all, that's my job. But they should challenge their advisers and take an active role in decision making. When it comes to investing and managing the relationship with an adviser, live by the dictum "trust, but verify." If the adviser is doing his or her job, if he or she is actively working to develop sound strategies on a client's behalf, he or she will welcome the challenge.

Or, as Warren Buffett once put it: "Wall Street is the only place that people ride to in a Rolls Royce to get advice from those who take the subway."[2]

The halo effect was first described by psychologist Edward Thorndike and is a cognitive bias in which we tend to give too much authority to people based on perceptions instead of real knowledge. Think about it this way. When you meet someone

---

[2]Andrew Goodman, "Top 40 Buffett-isms: Inspiration To Become A Better Investor," *Forbes*, September 25, 2013, www.forbes.com/sites/agoodman/2013/09/25/the-top-40-buffettisms-inspiration-to-become-a-better-investor.

with a PhD, you tend to think he or she has a great amount of intelligence. If you barely graduated from high school, you might be inclined to assume he or she is smarter than you. And if that person is smarter than you, he or she must know more about something than you could, right?

Wrong.

The halo effect is the reason anyone might take advice from someone on the radio calling himself, say, Dr. John. We assume he has more insight into relationships for a couple of reasons: 1) He has a radio show on which he dispenses relationship advice, and 2) He has "Dr." in front of his name. But do we really know anything about him? For instance, do we know he's really a doctor? I know someone with a PhD in mechanical engineering. He has every right to be referred to as "Dr." But does a strong grasp of calculus qualify him to dispense marriage advice? Not necessarily. He may be no more qualified than I am.

And what about the radio show? Isn't that proof that he knows what he's talking about? Well, if getting on the radio was about topical bona fides, then maybe. But the qualifications for being on the radio probably have more to do with being able to talk for hours on end and create appeal for advertisers than anything else.

It's the halo effect that leads to complacency when we talk about investing. We trust people because they work for a certain firm or have a certain degree. It's natural. As someone who works for a well-respected firm and worked hard for my degrees and professional qualifications, I certainly want those things to be appreciated, but it would be foolish to use them as a basis for simply taking my word for it.

Just as we will cover a bit later in the chapter about herds and the bandwagon effect (and how dangerous it can be to simply follow the crowd), it is dangerous to take someone's investment counsel at face value. Do the work. Challenge the logic and don't be afraid to get your hands dirty. After all, it

is your money, your savings, your retirement, your wealth—
you should work hard to make sure you feel confident in your
decisions.

Mistake 4: Information Overload

There are a lot of reasons to love the 24-hour news cycle and
the dissemination of digital media. You can keep tabs on the
world, discover new and interesting things, and feel more
connected to what's happening. But the major downside of our
always-on culture as it relates to investing is information overload. Investors who make decisions based on a talking-head
cable anchor will drive themselves crazy chasing the constant
flow of information. Flip on the TV at any time of day and you'll
be able to find people talking about companies—winners, losers, and all shades between. Stop. Switch to the History Channel
or, better yet, turn the TV off and read a book. Taking investment advice from a TV show host is like trying to find an organ
donation on Craigslist—a bad idea. Your financial adviser
has access to a lot more information than what's on TV and,
unlike the guy shouting about initial public offerings (IPOs) on
MSNBC whose job is to keep you watching, has a vested interest
in your long-term success. Develop the strategy that's right for
you and your goals and needs. Leave the stock chasing to the
day traders and rest a whole lot easier. The same goes for taking
advice from friends or coworkers who let you in on a "secret"
investment opportunity. Let them keep it a secret, and stick to
what's best for you.

In "When Less Is More: Simplification and the Art of
Investment,"[3] James Montier quotes Sir Arthur Conan Doyle
and his most famous character, Sherlock Holmes, as inspiration for those looking to limit their knowledge intake.

---

[3]James Montier, "When Less Is More: Simplification and the Art of Investment,"
www.designs.valueinvestorinsight.com/bonus/bonuscontent/docs/
Montier_12_07.pdf.

I consider that a man's brain originally is like a little empty attic, and you have to stock it with such furniture as you choose. A fool takes in all the lumber of every sort that he comes across, so that the knowledge which might be useful to him gets crowded out, or at best is jumbled up with a lot of other things, so that he has a difficulty laying his hands upon it. But the skillful workman is very careful indeed as to what he takes into his brain attic. He will have nothing but the tools, which may help him in doing his work, but of these he has a large assortment, and all in the most perfect order. It is a mistake to think that the little room has elastic walls and can distend to any extent. Depend on it; there comes a time when for every addition of knowledge, you forget something you knew before. It is of the highest importance, therefore, not to have useless facts elbowing out the useful ones.

Mistake 5: Mistaking Value and the Risk of Familiarity

During the dot-com bubble, people were getting rich overnight on IPOs for companies with little or no intrinsic value. Pets.com is, of course, one of the most famous examples and proved to be a harbinger of the inevitable burst that followed. But while things were going well and the markets continued to rise, it seemed like the sky was the limit. If you recall, Warren Buffett's philosophy of value investing was declared dead by the media, who seemed to usher in a new age of investment principles based on nothing more than a craze. We all know what happened. The bubble burst, and all those people who, months before, had been singing the dot-com praises lost most—if not all—of their capital. Warren Buffett, however, continued his ascension and remains one of the most successful investors of all time. How? He has maintained a clear focus on value over all else. This devotion to value kept him out of bubble markets, away from crowds, and sitting on the greatest portfolio the world has ever known. A lot of people mistake value for price. Value doesn't mean cheap. Value stocks may cost $1 a share or $200 a share. Price is not important. What is important, in terms of value, is the ratio of what the stock is trading for compared to what the company is worth. Too many investors chase returns instead of seeking value. Returns will eventually lead to a bubble and its inevitable burst. Value never loses for very long, at least. Stick to value strategies, like Buffett's or the 52-Week Low formula, and you'll find yourself on the right side of history with greater long-term returns and faster recovery times after markets take a dive.

Graham also believed that market valuations (stock prices) are often wrong. He used his famous "Mr. Market" parable to highlight a simple truth: stock prices will fluctuate substantially in value. His philosophy was that this feature of the market offers smart investors "an opportunity to buy wisely when prices fall sharply and to sell wisely when they advance a great deal."

The same goes for buying familiar companies. Too often, we allow familiarity to cloud our judgment as it relates to price. We see a company, we buy it, thinking it's a good deal for a company we have heard of, and overlook the fact that it was overpriced. This is why it is so important to distinguish between the System 1 thinking, which responds instantly to a stimulus, and System 2, which is measured and considered, as described in Daniel Kahneman's *Thinking, Fast and Slow.*[4] System 2 thinking may help to ground your decision to buy a familiar company simply because it is familiar.

A 2008 *Psychology Today* article[5] discussed the work of Chip Heath and Amos Tversky, who conducted a series

---

[4] Daniel Kahneman, *Thinking, Fast and Slow* (New York: Farrar, Straus and Giroux, 2011).
[5] John Nofsinger, "Familiarity Bias PART I: What Is It?" *Psychology Today* (*Mind on My Money* blog), July 25, 2008. www.psychologytoday.com/blog/mind-my-money/200807/familiarity-bias-part-i-what-is-it.

of experiments in which participants were presented a choice between two gambles: one unknown and one they were familiar with. Almost without fail, subjects picked the one with which they were more familiar, even when the odds of winning were lower. The same article cites the work of Gur Huberman, who argued that "familiarity is associated with a general sense of comfort with the known and discomfort with—even distaste for and fear of—the alien or distant."

How does the familiarity effect impact investment decisions? Quite simply, by limiting them to the familiar because familiar is often mistaken for better.

Mei Wang, a professor of finance at WHU-The Otto Beisheim School of Management in Germany, said the familiarity effect often leaves investors heavily under-diversified.[6] This means they only invest in companies they've heard of or in countries they live in. But, perhaps most dangerous is when investors over-invest or solely invest in the company they work for, which has a double risk. Should something catastrophic happen, these investors risk losing their employment income and the value of their savings all at once.

The 52-Week Low is designed to identify companies with value potential, regardless of familiarity. At any given time, it is comprised of 25 stocks. The 52-Week Low is designed to mitigate the risks that can come with familiarity. That's not to say, of course, that the companies on the list are necessarily unfamiliar, just that their familiarity has no bearing on the decision to include them.

Understanding the common biases, effects, and mistakes investors make is the first step to avoiding them and is the basis of a systematic, disciplined, approach that overcomes human emotions, instincts, and frailties to mitigate risk and maximize long-term value.

---

[6]Robert Stammers, "Three Behavioral Biases That Can Affect Your Investment Performance," *Forbes*, December 21, 2011, www.forbes.com/sites/cfainstitute/2011/12/21/three-behavioral-biases-that-can-affect-your-investment-performance.

CHAPTER 5

Filter 2: Free Cash Flow Yield

*J*acobian Inverse: *If I wanted to help ensure that my stock investment bears the risk of equity ownership but pays me less cash than the risk-free cash from a 10-year Treasury bond, then I would definitely buy companies whose free cash flow yield is in line with or less than the risk-free rate. This would help to ensure that I am buying overvalued businesses.*

This leads to the correct strategy, which is to set a requirement that any company worth investing in must provide a cash flow multiple over the risk-free rate. This helps to ensure that we are buying a business with a margin of safety.

The second of the five filters that go into the 52-Week Low formula helps us determine whether a company is worth investing in at all. While the first filter was used to determine the potential for a company to remain competitive over the long haul, the second filter forces us to take a look under the hood, so to speak, to determine a company's value as an owner and whether that potential cash flow is great enough to warrant the risk of investing in the company at all.

When it comes to buying a stock, you really want to look at your purchase as an investment in an actual business. This advice is reinforced within the book *The Intelligent Investor*, written by Benjamin Graham,[1] specifically in the "Margin of Safety" chapter, where he discusses that investing is most intelligent when it is most businesslike. To sum up the chapter, he states:

> It is amazing to see how many capable businessmen try to operate on Wall Street with complete disregard of all the sound principles through which they have gained success in their own undertakings. Yet every corporate security may best be viewed, in the first instance, as an ownership interest in, or a claim against, a specific business enterprise. And if a person sets out to make profits from security purchases and sales, he is embarking on a business venture of his own, which must be run in accordance with accepted business principles if it is to have a chance of success.

So, what is free cash flow?

Let's first define the term. I believe free cash flow, owner earnings, and distributable cash flow are all synonymous. Distributable cash flow, as defined by Bruce Greenwald and Paul Sonkin in their book *Value Investing from Graham to Buffett and Beyond*,[2] is the money the owners can extract from the firm and still leave its operations intact.

Why is free cash flow so important in the evaluation process? Research has shown that free cash flow is less susceptible to accounting manipulations than reported net income.

"The income statement gives the company's accounting profit; the cash flow statement reports what happened to its money," according to Graham and Dodd's *Security Analysis*.[3] It continues to say, "Companies that try to cook the books such as

[1] Benjamin Graham, *The Intelligent Investor* (New York: Harper & Brothers, 1949). Quoted passage comes from page 523 of the Revised Edition (Collins Business, 2006).
[2] Bruce C. N. Greenwald, Judd Kahn, Paul D. Sonkin, and Michael van Biema, *Value Investing: From Graham to Buffett and Beyond* (Hoboken, NJ: John Wiley & Sons, 2004).
[3] Benjamin Graham and David L. Dodd, *Security Analysis, Sixth Edition* (New York: McGraw Hill, 2008).

Enron or Waste Management can always dress up the earnings statement, at least for a while. But they can't manufacture cash."

Or, as investment firm Manning & Napier put it in the white paper "Free Cash Flow and Dividends: How a Focus on Yield Can Help Investors":

> While earnings figures on a company's income statement can often be distorted through the use of accruals, depreciation and by capitalizing expenditures, free cash flow generally avoids these pitfalls as it is very difficult for companies to hide how much cash they take in for a given period. The bankruptcy of the Enron Corporation may be the most egregious example of free cash flow raising red flags about a company's financial health. In the 15 quarters prior to their bankruptcy in 2001, Enron posted 14 quarters with positive earnings per share, but only 5 quarters with positive free cash flow per share.[4]

But it's important to differentiate free cash flow yield from the enterprise value of a company. Enterprise value is what it would cost you to buy the entire company (Equity + Debt − Cash). For example, as of December 10, 2013, the market capitalization of Caterpillar Inc. is $54.99 billion, while its enterprise value is $88.16 billion (Table 5.1).[5]

Table 5.1   An Example in Calculating Enterprise Value

Valuation Measures

Market Cap (intraday)	54.99 billion
Enterprise Value (Dec. 10, 2013)	88.16 billion
Trailing P/E (TTM, intraday)	16.47
Forward P/E (FYE Dec. 31, 2014)	14.87

Data provided by Capital IQ, except where noted.

---

[4] Available at https://www.manning-napier.com/Portals/0/documents/insights/white-papers/free-cash-flow-dividends.pdf.
[5] Data from http://finance.yahoo.com/q/ks?s=CAT+Key+Statistics.

So this means that Caterpillar has roughly $33 billion in debt. When you a buy a business in the real world, you not only buy the shares from the existing shareholders, but you also inherit the debt obligation as well. This is why only looking at a company's price-to-earnings (P/E) multiple can be misleading because it does not include the debt side of the business. In fact, you will hear terms like *earnings yield*, which is a company's P/E ratio inverted. So if you have a company with a P/E of 20, its earnings yield is 1/20, which is 5 percent.

To take the Caterpillar example a step further, what would be its P/E ratio when you include debt? Its P/E would be approximately 25.2, and its earnings yield would be 1/25.2, which is 3.95 percent.

Let's take a look at owner earnings, also known as free cash flow.

Of all the landmarks Warren Buffett has established for the world of investing, few can compare in terms of lasting importance to a single paragraph in his 1986 letter to the shareholders of Berkshire Hathaway:

> [Owner earnings] represent a) reported earnings plus b) depreciation, depletion, amortization, and certain other non-cash charges . . . less c) the average annual amount of capitalized expenditures for plant and equipment, etc. that the business requires to fully maintain its long-term competitive position and its unit volume.

It's a mouthful, to be sure, but Buffett changed the way many investors think with that deft stroke of his pen by essentially saying that considering investments as purchasing a small or large portion of a company does not give a clear enough picture of the value of that company. Rather, investors—or at least he and those at Berkshire Hathaway—should judge investments as if they are purchasing the entire company. Owner earnings is an approach that asks investors to consider the value of a company should it be purchased outright.

"If all you have is a hammer, everything looks like a nail," Chris Davis, of the Davis New York Venture Fund, told Morningstar's David Kathman, CFA, in 1999.[6] Davis was explaining why he preferred using owner's earnings over other traditional measures of P/E. The measurement, he said, gives a better measure of a stock's true value. It is a more sophisticated measurement, which takes into account all costs (including stock options) to determine the real earnings potential of a company.

Here's how I, and many well-known investors, calculate free cash flow:

Operating Cash Flow − Capital Costs of Maintaining Current Capacity = Free Cash Flow

So, free cash flow is what the business owner could take out of the cash register while still ensuring that the company is staying competitive (the deduction of the capital costs). Free cash flow is only part of the equation.

The next part of the equation is to find the enterprise value of the business.

Market Capitalization + Debt − Cash = Enterprise Value

And free cash flow yield:

Free Cash Flow/ Enterprise Value = Free Cash Flow Yield

---

[6]David Kathman, "Putting a Price Tag on Slippery Stocks," Morningstar, May 7, 1999, http://news.morningstar.com/articlenet/article.aspx?id=754.

So, if you had a business with a market cap of $10 but debt of $90, the enterprise value would be $100. If the business generates $1 in free cash flow, then its free cash flow yield is $1/$100, or 1 percent.

Understanding and calculating the free cash flow yield of a company gives you a sense of how *good* of an investment it is in real cash return versus what you could receive owning a risk-free Treasury bond.

If Treasury bonds provide an investment yield of 3 percent and the free cash flow yield of the above company is 1 percent, then why take the risk? Why invest in a company, which is fraught with risk in the form of catastrophe, economic downturn, competitive forces, scandal, and such, when you can make three times as much guaranteed by investing in a Treasury bond?

The answer is simple: You wouldn't.

There has to be a margin of safety if you are going to take on the risk of stock ownership. The margin of safety is the free cash flow yield multiple over the risk-free rate. Benjamin Graham's *The Intelligent Investor* has a chapter titled "Margin of Safety," in which you'll find the following footnote, summarizing the discussion that followed a lecture he gave in 1972.

> The margin of safety is the difference between the percentage rate of the earnings on the stock at the price you pay for it and the rate of interest on bonds, and that margin of safety is the difference which would absorb unsatisfactory developments. At the time the 1965 edition of *The Intelligent Investor* was written, the typical stock was selling at 11 times earnings, giving about 9 percent return as against 4 percent on bonds. In that case you had a margin of safety of over 100 percent.

Take, for instance, the following examples:

You have the opportunity to buy one ice cream truck.

The red truck generates $1,000 in free cash flow and has market capitalization of $10,000. So the red truck has a P/E of 10.

The green truck generates $750 in free cash flow and has a market capitalization of $15,000. So the green truck has a P/E of 20.

Which truck do you think most investors would choose?

After doing a little more homework, we discover that the red truck has $20,000 in long-term debt. With this knowledge you now realize you would need $30,000 to buy the entire business ($10,000 + $20,000). So the free cash flow yield of this business is 3.33 percent. This is barely above the risk-free rate of a 10-year Treasury bond.

After doing a similar analysis on the green truck, we learn that it has $10,000 in cash and no debt. All we would need to buy this business is $5,000 ($15,000 − $10,000). So the free cash flow yield of this business is 15 percent. This business is earning in real cash five times more than the risk-free rate.

Which business should you buy or has the greatest margin of safety?

A businessman—which is what you are, or are becoming—would buy the green truck. Why? Because you are earning 15 percent on your investment that you can reinvest in the business or have distributed out to you. You want to compare this free cash flow yield of 15 percent to what you could earn on a risk-free 10-year Treasury. If the 10-year Treasury is paying 2.75 percent, then you are earning more than 5 times more owning the green truck over a 10-year Treasury. This creates a substantial margin of safety. The red truck, on the other hand, is earning less than twice that of the 10-year Treasury and would not be worth the risk.

Remember: The free cash flow yield multiple over the 10-year Treasury bond is known as the margin of safety.

If you are going to take on the risk of purchasing a company, the free cash flow yield needs to be more than slightly larger than a 10-year Treasury bond. For the 52-Week Low formula, we set a minimum free cash flow yield multiple over the risk-free rate of a 10-year Treasury bond. We don't want to earn slightly more. We want to earn a lot more in cash over the 10-year treasury, given the risks inherent in investing in common stocks. And while the specific minimum hurdle rate or multiplier is proprietary, it is important to realize that using a multiplier—rather than a simple more-or-less measurement—helps to not only increase potential reward but to mitigate risk by focusing on the companies with a high margin of safety.

Free cash flow yield couples the health of the company (free cash flow) with its valuation (enterprise value), much like ROIC over WACC is a key indicator of incremental shareholder value. That's why these are early filters in determining the right companies to go into the 52-Week Low formula. These early filters help ensure that the companies we invest in have solid potential for real value, that they are less subject to or more capable of negotiating violent market swings, and represent investments worth the risk.

Bruce Berkowitz, the founder of Fairholme Capital Management and recipient of Morningstar's Domestic-Stock Fund Manager of the Decade award, discussed in Fairholme's September 30, 2009, Webcast the importance of owner earnings and free cash flow and how it helped him avoid the dot-com bubble, among other risks:

At Fairholme, we treat common stock as the most junior bond in a company's capital structure, where the true earnings, the free cash flow of a company, are akin to a coupon without a maturity date. We get really excited when we can find more senior and secure bonds that yield better than average equity-like returns. We then compare market prices to our estimates of free cash flows, to determine an expected return on investment. Price matters, and buying right is half the battle. Getting a reasonable estimate of expected free cash flow is the other half.[7]

If all you used during the rise and fall of the dot-com era was this metric, which uses free cash flow as the numerator, then you would have avoided most—if not all—of the businesses that went bankrupt during the fall. The reason you would have avoided these companies is that this metric only identifies companies that have positive free cash flow. Many of the businesses coming into the market during this cycle had zero or negative free cash flow.

Earlier in the book, in the "Story of a Dollar" case study, you saw how the 52-Week Low strategy underperformed in the late 1990s. Most investors were disregarding fundamental valuation metrics during this time period. That trend reversed dramatically when the bubble burst, whereby the outperformance started favoring the strategy when valuations and logical decision-making became important again to the investment process.

Remember: Think like a business owner, just as Warren Buffett, Benjamin Graham, and many other highly-esteemed investors recommend, and look at companies that have a margin of safety. Would a highly-regarded businessman buy a business that pays him less cash than a risk-free Treasury bond?

No, and neither should you.

---

[7]Transcript available at www.grahamanddoddsville.net/wordpress/Files/Gurus/ Bruce Berkowitz/Fairholme Conference Call - 09-30-09.pdf.

Case Study: The 52-Week Low and Its Recovery

Jacobian Inverse: *I will concentrate solely on growth without regard to value and will pay any price for that hopeful growth. I will assume the market will continue to climb and have faith that, despite evidence to the contrary, catastrophic loss is a thing of the past. I will tie the strategy of my investments to what is currently performing the best rather than make choices that should help insulate me from downside risk and allow for quicker recovery. I will not think about recovery and focus only on infinite gain.*

This time is never different. Accept this as a fact. It's vital that you do, and it will make all the difference to the overall health and long-term value of your investments if you accept a few unerring facts about the market:

1. Things will get better.
2. Things will get worse.
3. There is no such thing as a sure way of knowing when and where each will be the case.
4. So you'd better plan for the worst, not the best.

It's that simple.

To some, preparing for the worst means sticking their head in the sand or thinking happy thoughts. For others, it means avoidance. For the 52-Week Low investor, it should mean sticking to your strategy. There are a lot of things that can cause a market collapse: natural disaster, political failure, crisis, war, and so on. But there are only a few things that can ensure a disaster will get worse and they are all avoidable: fear, anger, and panic.

I'm not saying that an investor should be a robot or something less than human. Quite the opposite. What I'm arguing is that an investment strategy should recognize emotions for what they are—distractions to good decision making—and provide structure to work around them, in spite of them.

At the time I'm writing this (late fall 2013), the sky looks blue and endless for investors. The headlines each night announce new record highs for the Standard & Poor's (S&P) and Dow, and the talking heads on television are chanting a new era of prosperity; unemployment is finally falling and it seems like the world is an investor's oyster.

We all ought to know better, and some of us (all of us, subconsciously) do.

We know this time won't be different. We know eventually the gains will begin to plateau. We know they will slide. We know there is a significant possibility that they will fall faster than an apple in Newton's yard. How do we know this? Because history suggests they will. Just 18 months ago, those same talking heads and headlines were reporting violent three-digit swings in the market in the period between lunch and close. Not long before that, we seemed to watch helplessly as the market tumbled. That time, it was the real estate bubble. Before that, it was the dot-com boom and bust. Before that, inflation, the Cold War, trouble in the Middle East. Each and every time, the sky fell and, eventually, seemed endless.

If you get anything out of the 52-Week Low, it should be this: Don't listen to the headlines for investing advice. Don't listen to your friends' hysteria or their defeat. Or listen but be ready to forget everything you hear—hope, fear, or otherwise. Because, at the end of the day, any day, the dusk is the same. This time is never different.

A favorite saying of mine is that it doesn't matter how many times you fall. What matters is how many times you get back up. Recovery and resilience aren't about avoiding problems, burying your head in the sand, or losing it in the clouds. Recovery is about having the skills and strategies in place to recover when times get tough and do it as quickly and completely as possible.

The years 2007 to 2009 were the worst period in recent memory—33 years to be exact. Between November 2007 and February 2009, the S&P 500 was on a 16-month free fall, losing more than 50 percent of its value. Triple digit single-day losses in the Dow were common, and investors and financial professionals were on a roller coaster of loss and recovery. I remember it clearly: everyone was scrambling to stop the bleeding and wondering when the other shoe was going to drop. It was a bad time to be in my business, a bad time, in fact, to be in most businesses.

I would be lying—to you and myself—if I said the 52-Week Low formula was immune to the Great Recession. It was not. Like every other strategy, mine took its lumps.[8]

In 16 months, the S&P 500 lost more than 50 percent of its value, and in the same amount of time, the 52-Week Low lost 45.4 percent.

---

[8]According to independent back-testing by Empiritrage, LLC.

(continued)

(*continued*)

It was an absolutely brutal time to be invested in anything. It's completely natural to allow fear and panic to set in when the prognosis looks like this. I know I certainly did, but this is only half the story. Recovery follows loss, but recovery is almost always misunderstood by investors. Full recovery is not achieved when the percentage gained is equal to the percentage lost. Rather, proportionately, recovery requires greater positive performance than loss.

If you had a dollar and I took 50 percent, you'd be left with $0.50. You can't add 50 percent to be made whole again. That would only be $0.25. You'd need a 100 percent recovery to get back to where you started, before I took your money. This is the danger of percentages when talking about recovery in the media. They can be terribly deceiving and equally as difficult to follow and understand.

- A 10 percent loss requires an 11.11 percent recovery.
- A 20 percent loss requires a 25 percent recovery.
- A 33.24 percent loss requires a 49.76 percent recovery.
- A 50.95 percent loss, like the one suffered by the S&P 500, requires a 103.97 percent recovery.

As you can see, every percentage point counts.

Getting investors back to where they started before the recession required twice the percentage growth that it had lost in 16 months. It was going to take years, they said at the time, and for most it did. Several times, there were stops and starts. Recovery would begin and then falter. Headlines would inspire fear. Market rushes would lead to violent swings. The Information Age went into overdrive at about the same time the economy tanked and bottomed out. People were scared and acting responsively. Complete recovery was challenging, to say the least.

But the 52-Week Low, which focuses on identifying quality companies with more sellers than buyers—companies primed for growth and better insulated from loss—not only mitigated a portion of the losses but led to a much faster recovery than the market. Recovery looked something like the chart shown in Figure 5.1.

The 52-Week Low hit its bottom and bounced back to even in just 12 months. Sixteen months of losses were made up in two 6-month resetting cycles. The S&P got back to even in March 2012, a recovery time of 37 months.

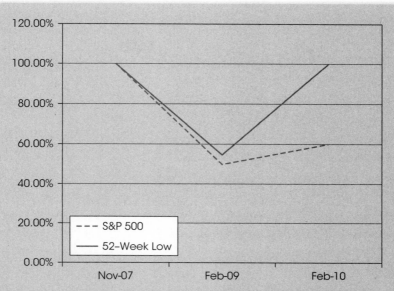

**Figure 5.1   Recovery Following the "Great Recession of 2008":
52-Week Low versus S&P 500**

This is a compelling finding and emblematic of how my mind
works. Rather than focusing on strategies with disproportionate
upsides, the strategy helped me control and protect wealth by focusing on the worst-case scenario. The period between November 2007
and February 2009 was that worst-case scenario. In 33 years of back-
testing, this period was the single worst performing for both the S&P
and the 52-Week Low.

The 52-Week Low has proven its resilience time and again. In fact,
of all the data reviewed by independent analysis firm Empiritrage,
LLC, the only main comparison metric where the 52-Week Low underperformed the S&P was in the worst absolute return month metric.
In November 1987, the 52-Week Low lost 25.84 percent, while the
S&P 500 lost 21.58 percent. However, the 52-Week Low best absolute
return month was 32.06 percent, versus 13.52 percent for the S&P.

Continuing the analysis of the downside, here are some other
telling findings that demonstrate the way the 52-Week Low strategy
protected investments by insulating against losses.

(continued)

(*continued*)

    Worst 12-month performance:
        S&P 500: −42.54 percent
        52-Week Low: −37.39 percent

    Worst 36-month performance:
        S&P 500: −40.35%
        52-Week Low: −31.22%

    Number of losing years between 1980 and 2012:

        S&P 500: 6
        52-Week Low: 4

The reason the 52-Week Low is able to mitigate loss and quickly aid recovery is the same as the reason it outperforms the market on the upside: regular and regimented rebalancing of the 25 stocks that make up the strategy. The 52-Week Low is rebalanced twice a year for retirement accounts, and typically once a year for large non-retirement accounts due to the taxation of short-term capital gains versus long-term capital gains. This rebalancing, while focusing on undervalued companies primed for recovery, means not riding losses for very long and increasing the likelihood that companies will be growing aggressively before the market catches up.

Here's how the 52-Week Low performed before costs against the S&P from 1980 to 2012, taking into account both annual and biannual rebalancing of New York Stock Exchange (NYSE) stocks with 20 percent, 40 percent, and 60 percent minimum market capitalization:

Annual Rebalance
    20 percent minimum market capitalization of NYSE stocks:
        52-Week Low: 14.2 percent
        S&P 500: 11.36 percent

    40 percent minimum market capitalization of NYSE stocks:
        52-Week Low: 15.99 percent
        S&P 500: 11.36 percent

    60 percent minimum market capitalization of NYSE stocks:
        52-Week Low: 16.12 percent
        S&P 500: 11.36 percent

Semiannual Rebalance

20 percent minimum market capitalization of NYSE stocks:
    52-Week Low: 14.69 percent
    S&P 500: 11.36 percent

40 percent minimum market capitalization of NYSE stocks:
    52-Week Low: 15.89 percent
    S&P 500: 11.36 percent

60 percent minimum market capitalization of NYSE stocks:
    52-Week Low: 17.17 percent
    S&P 500: 11.36 percent

Why is the additional analysis needed? This is important for those with sizable non–individual retirement arrangement (IRA) accounts to see what the returns look like if you rebalance every 12 months versus every 6 months. Both back tests show an incremental return for semiannual rebalancing, but when you factor in the short-term gain tax implications, you could possibly fare better on an after-tax return basis by rebalancing every 12 months. So this strategy can work for both non-IRA investors rebalancing every 12 months and retirement plan investors choosing to rebalance every 6 months.

The 52-Week Low has proven itself resilient and able to sustain during periods of calamity while giving investors a strategy to take advantage of periods of market growth. And when it comes to investing, the most important thing to know is that this time is never different. Don't plan for the boom times. Plan for the worst-case scenario and be ready to capitalize in times of growth.

6

The Power of Fear and Decision Fatigue

*J*acobian Inverse: *So that I don't suffer any anxiety, fear, or uncertainty, I will invest only in investments that I am excited about and where there is an abundance of capital. It feels a lot better investing in companies that everyone likes and that have done well rather than buying businesses that no one likes and are doing poorly. I don't want to feel uncomfortable in the investment process at all.*

This inversion should help you realize that if you are feeling concerned or uncomfortable and you're in a cognitive battle, you may be buying a business at the right price. Remember, when you buy low, the news, the enthusiasm and your emotions surrounding the business are not good.

Let's play a little game. Let's say I gave you $25 to bid on an item at an auction. It's a small item, but I told you that if you won the auction, you could keep whatever was left over from the original $25. How aggressively would you bid? Probably not that hard. It's not your money after all. But what if I gave you $25 and told you the only way to keep it was to win the auction? Would that change your perspective? Would you bid harder because not winning would cost you $25?

Well, science tells us that the answer to this last question is a resounding *yes*.

Scientists at New York University conducted a very similar study in 2008, using imaging technology to study brain activity among people given a lottery ticket and those given money to bid at an auction. The lottery folks—those who could gain only from winning—were far less interested (as seen in their brain activity) than those who stood to lose money if they didn't win an auction. The difference? Fear.

Fear is one of the most powerful forces in the human experience. Fear keeps you sharp. It can keep you alive. You can see the power of fear in the lives of the people you know. Imagine the most successful people in your life. They are probably the people least motivated by fear. They take chances. They try new things. They are willing to think outside the box. What about the least successful? They probably don't switch jobs or learn new skills because they are afraid of something—the work it will take, the unknown results. Fear can be crippling. It can be stifling. And, as it relates to your investments, it can prevent you from meeting your goals, or worse, from making the right decisions.

So how do you overcome fear? By removing it from the equation. Trying to focus on the positive—winning the lottery will benefit me more than losing an auction will hurt me—is too difficult. Besides, the opposite of fear is not optimism, it's logic, and logic-based decisions often require assistance.

I have a friend who prefers to drive on long trips because he is afraid to fly. Fear keeps him grounded. It doesn't matter that he's statistically safer in the air than on the highways and byways of America. And it doesn't matter that driving can be more expensive and time consuming. He has fully submitted to his fear of getting on an airplane and will thus never do it—not alone, anyway. But what if his wife made the decision for him? What if she studied the statistics and logistics and helped him get on a plane? Fear, for the most part, thrives on solitude. It's a completely personal experience and often is unfounded.

How does this relate to your investing? Well, removing fear should be the basis of your relationship with your financial adviser. It's his or her job to study the data and make logical recommendations. If you want to succeed with your investments, your job is to find a way to mute fear enough to be able to listen, ask questions to understand the logic, and make good decisions.

If you had a dollar and had to make a choice between investing it in something that will ensure you will lose no more than 10 percent, but will not make you more than 5 percent, or a strategy that had a 75 percent probability of making you 22 percent but may lose you 15 percent, what would you do? If you are the kind of person who makes fear-based decisions, you'll take the first one. But if you are someone who can overcome fear to make logical decisions, you understand that the second scenario is better and take it. Still, most people will take the first because of the power of fear. It feels safer, more concrete. Pursuing any other strategy feels too unknown, too risky.

But fear often has nothing to do with reality.

Respected research firm Dalbar conducted a 10-year study[1] on "destructive investor behavior" and concluded that most investors are "driven by emotions like fear and greed"; they succumbed to negative behavior like:

- Pouring money into top performers, expecting winning streaks to go on.
- Avoiding underperforming areas of the market, expecting recovery to never happen.
- Abandoning their investment plans and trying to time moves to the market.

---

[1] "Quantitative Analysis of Investor Behavior," March 2012, available at www.qaib.com.

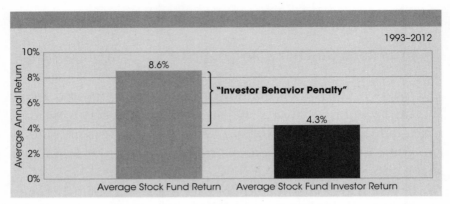

Figure 6.1   Average Stock Fund Return versus Average Stock Fund Investor Return

The results, according to Dalbar, are pretty striking. Between 1993 and 2012, the average stock return was 8.6 percent, while the average stock fund investor earned 4.3 percent. The difference—the disparity between real-world performance and investor realization of gains—amounts to what Davis Advisors[2] refers to as an "investor behavior penalty." In other words, investors penalized their own performance through bad behavior, which was usually driven by fear or greed (Figure 6.1).

It's why most people invest alongside everyone else—it gives a false sense of safety. To them, it's better not to run the risk of looking different and lose. It feels safer, more concrete. Pursuing any other strategy feels too unknown, too risky.

In our childhoods, when we became fearful or afraid of something, we would seek out information to disprove our feelings of fear or question where our fear is coming from.

---

[2]Davis Advisors, "Essential Wisdom for Today's Market," http://davisfunds.com/downloads/EW.pdf.

As adults, it seems we have forgotten this process from our youth. We must remember to apply that same energy and persistence in challenging our deeply held fears of investing to help avoid its pitfalls or miss logical opportunities.

And if you still aren't convinced, I have a question for you:

In the United States, what is more likely to cause your untimely demise: a shark attack or falling airplane parts?

Well, if you've made it this far into the book, I assume you know the correct answer: falling airplane parts.

According to psychologist Daniel Kahneman, author of *Thinking, Fast and Slow*, you are 30 times more likely to be killed by falling airplane parts than by a shark attack.[3] So why, then, aren't we all constantly afraid of death by debris? Or why is it that we've all got that tingling in our spine whenever we step into the ocean?

Fear—illogical, irrational fear. We've all seen *Jaws* and *Soul Surfer*. The mystique of shark attacks is great in this country, and thus our fear is as well. We have more information—fictional or not—about shark attacks and therefore perceive the danger as being much higher.

Fear often has nothing to do with actual risk. Risk is a logical calculation, not an emotional one. Don't make fear-based decisions with your investments. Instead, create or follow rules that mitigate risk while giving you a better chance at reward.

In August 2011, the *New York Times Magazine* published a story by journalist John Tierney[4] detailing the fate of three men up for parole in an Israeli prison. Of the three, only one was set free. Do you think you can guess which one?

---

[3] See www.learner.org/series/discoveringpsychology/11/e11expand.html.
[4] John Tierney, "Do You Suffer from Decision Fatigue?" *New York Times Magazine*, August 21 2001, www.nytimes.com/2011/08/21/magazine/do-you-suffer-from-decision-fatigue.html?pagewanted=all&_r=0.

Case 1 (heard at 8:50 A.M.): An Arab Israeli serving a 30-month sentence for fraud.

Case 2 (heard at 3:10 P.M.): A Jewish Israeli serving a 16-month sentence for assault.

Case 3 (heard at 4:25 P.M.): An Arab Israeli serving a 30-month sentence for fraud.

All the information you need to know to figure out which case resulted in a parole is contained in those brief case descriptions. But do you recognize it? If you follow the news, particularly the news about Israel, you probably have some preconceived notions based upon ethnicity or type of crime. If so, you might think a non-violent crime—fraud—would be more likely to yield a parole than the violent crime of assault. But two of the cases involved fraud and only one was paroled. What about ethnicity? Do you assume that the Jewish prisoner would be more likely to get paroled than an Arab prisoner because of the complicated ethnic politics of the region?

Both lines of thinking make sense, on the surface anyway. But the critical data reveals that which prisoner was paroled may have had nothing to do with the nature of the crime or the ethnicity of the prisoner, but rather the time of day. The prisoner that was paroled was Case 1—the first case heard in the day.

But why is that?

Decision fatigue is something we all face. In a world where we are constantly bombarded with information and data, a world where our lives are shaped not just by the few big decisions we make, but by the thousands of tiny decisions we make every day. And the longer the day goes on, the more decisions we have to make. By the end of the day, we have made hundreds—if not thousands—of decisions, each based on a piece or pieces of data, all considered, all taken into account. And as the day, which was fresh and new in the morning, comes to a close, we are simply tired of making them.

It's the reason so many of us sit on the couch at night and watch whatever is on television; the reason small items like candy and trash magazines are placed at the register in the grocery store. By the time we get to that point in the shopping experience, we are tired of making considered decisions. We have spent time in the produce aisle, at the dairy case, the meat counter, and in the dry goods aisles. We have made decisions based on our needs and our health and by the time we get to the counter, grabbing a candy bar seems fine—a no-brainer, literally. It's the same reason the prisoner in the first case of the morning at that particular Israeli prison had the best shot at receiving parole. By the end of the day, the parole board had made hundreds of decisions—big and small—and it was bound to take the easiest course of action: leaving convicted criminals in jail.

In 2004, MIT's Dan Ariely and Jiwoong Shin published the results of a study they conducted titled, "Keeping Doors Open: The Effect of Unavailability on the Incentives to Keep Options Viable."[5] The study, which was based on a computer game Ariely designed, created two groups of players. The website *Reflective Happiness*[6] recounts the game this way:

> Clicking on one door took the participant into a room, and clicking inside the room gave the participant a certain amount of money. The amount of money varied randomly within some range, and that range depended on the room. At any time, the participant could also move to another room with one click. Thus, the game created a tradeoff between earning money (clicking in a room) and finding the best source of money (switching rooms). This was the "constant-availability" group.

---

[5]Jiwoong Shin and Dan Ariely, "Keeping Doors Open: The Effect of Unavailability on the Incentives to Keep Options Viable," *Management Science* 2004, 50:575–586, http://web.mit.edu/ariely/www/MIT/Papers/doors.pdf.
[6]"The Hidden Cost of Keeping Your Options Open," *Reflective Happiness*, December 23, 2012, http://reflectivehappiness.wordpress.com/2012/12/23/the-hidden-cost-of-keeping-your-options-open/#more-277.

In the "decreased-availability" group, participants played a modified version of this game. In this version . . . **there was an added potential cost of losing options**.

In the end . . . the takeaway from this is that **humans have a natural tendency to want to keep options open, which leads to suboptimal outcomes**.

In the aforementioned study, Shin and Ariely also stated, "In a world where maintaining options has no cost, such a tendency would have been nonconsequential. However, we believe that in most day-to-day cases, there is substantial cost to keeping options open, which would lead to erroneous behavior."

Decision fatigue is a major culprit in making poor investment choices. We are awash in information. We research and study options and, eventually, we get tired, complacent, and even a bit lazy. We take the path of least resistance, make ill-considered choices, and select investments impulsively.

Just as the structure of the 52-Week Low is designed to eliminate noise and keep us focused on value, so too is it designed to countermand decision fatigue. The five filters of the formula eliminate thousands of potential investments from consideration, allowing you to use your mental energy to make the right decisions. These filters, like a checklist, keep us focused on what really matters. Can you imagine if a pilot didn't have a preflight checklist? She might wander aimlessly around the plane, checking gauges at random, filling her capacity for processing data with meaningless distractions and creating the potential to miss the most important items that will keep her and her passengers safe.

There's comfort in that process, in the focus of a system. That comfort goes a long way to combating the fear that can arise from too much information, from trying to take it all in and inevitably making the wrong decision because you are tired or because you want to have as many options as possible. Systems give us clarity and focus and may prevent us from making the wrong choice because of information overload or decision fatigue.

7

Filter 3: Return on Invested Capital

*J*acobian Inverse: *I want to seek out and invest in industries and companies that have a knack for generating returns on capital less than their cost of capital. This will increase my chances of losing my total investment over time due to the erosion of shareholder value.*

This leads to the correct way of thinking. If I want to increase the probability of compounding my investment, I will look at industries and companies that not only generate returns on capital over their cost of capital currently but have a knack for generating returns on capital in excess of their cost of capital over 10 years.

For a business to pass this filter it must achieve a minimum return on invested capital (ROIC) to ensure that the company is earning more than its cost of capital (COC). I am interested in identifying businesses that generate ROIC greater than their current COC. I also then study their long-term ROIC results to ensure that the company in question has a knack for achieving ROIC greater than its COC over a 10-year cycle.

The concept of ROIC is quite intuitive, as it is the percentage return an investor earns on his invested capital in the company. However, ROIC does not mean much unless you compare it to a company's COC. If a company is earning 12 percent ROIC and its COC is 10 percent, it is said to be adding economic value. If a company's COC is 9 percent and its ROIC is 7 percent, it is said to be destroying economic value because every dollar being invested is earning less than the required rate of return of its investors. This evaluation process is known as the *economic value added approach,* or EVA, among investment bankers and other business evaluators.

> **ROIC > COC = Passes the third filter and moves on to filter 4.**
>
> **ROIC < COC = Fails the third filter and is disregarded.**

How would using ROIC as one of your screens have avoided losing all your money on WorldCom? What was WorldCom's ROIC during the years leading up to its bankruptcy?

Gretchen Morgenson wrote about WorldCom in the *New York Times*:

> An extreme example of a company that had returns on invested capital that were below its cost of capital is WorldCom, the telecommunications darling that collapsed in 2002. According to *Foundations of Economic Value Added,* a book by James L. Grant, from 1993 to 2000 return on invested capital at WorldCom ranged from, 2.23 percent to a high of 9.5 percent, but the company's cost of capital was more than 10 percent throughout this time. For much of that time period, WorldCom's stock price was rising.
>
> WorldCom, of course, was in a category by itself. But the message is clear: a stock price does not always reflect real economic value. Van Clieaf labels these kinds of companies "value myths" because on the surface they are producing gains for shareholders but underneath they

are generating negative returns on their investments in plants, equipment, acquisitions or other items.[1]

The *Journal of Forensic Accounting* published an article in 2004 titled "Lessons for Auditors: Quantitative and Qualitative Red Flags." In it, WorldCom and Enron are used as examples of how stock price can send a conflicting value message and how both firms' ROIC were clear indicators that something was amiss.

Leading up to the major implosions that rocked both companies, there were signs of trouble. Enron's and WorldCom's returns on assets were 1.49 percent and 1.33 percent, respectively, according to the Journal, while industry benchmarks ranged from 8 percent to 12 percent. The companies' returns on equity were 8.54 percent and 2.39 percent, while benchmarks were between 9 percent and 16 percent.

But perhaps most telling were the two firms' low ROIC compared to cost of capital. They were experiencing returns on invested capital of 7 percent while the cost of capital was 12 percent, meaning it cost them more to borrow than what they would make. These should have been clear warning signs.

Remember: ROIC < COC = Fails the test and is disregarded. We are interested only in businesses that create incremental shareholder value.

We live in the age of the celebrity CEO. It seems like every day there's a new memoir, a new television special, a new name on the lips of every American. It's nothing new. Go back to the early days of the twentieth century and names like Rockefeller, Chase, and Ford were as famous as names like Babe Ruth and Charlie Chaplin. In the 1980s, it was Lee Iacocca. The 1990s were all about Jack Welch and Bill Gates. The millennium belonged to Steve Jobs. Now, people flutter at names like Mark Zuckerberg and Jeff Bezos.

---

[1] Gretchen Morgenson, "When the Stock Price Hides Trouble," *New York Times,* October 12, 2013, www.nytimes.com/2013/10/13/business/when-the-stock-price-hides-trouble.html.

Business has always had its share of the famous and the rich, the rock star visionaries, innovators, entrepreneurs, and leaders. These are people we look up to, people we admire, people we love, and people we love to hate. But, too often, we confuse the cult of celebrity CEO personality with management. Vision is not the same thing as stewardship. Innovation is not the same thing as good decision making.

Just as I shy away from crowds when it comes to investing, I shy away from celebrity when it comes to assessing how well a company is managed. To confuse one for the other is to find yourself walking into a classic investing pitfall: the herding bias. If there's one thing investors who follow the 52-Week Low formula hate, it's a herd. They want to find opportunities where no one else is looking and take advantage of opportunities to invest in undervalued companies with great potential for growth. You can't do that in the middle of a feeding frenzy. And if everyone you know is abuzz about a CEO, then his company might as well be a rodeo.

Management matters in every case, but especially when you follow a strategy like the 52-Week Low. Value strategies require investors to look at the long-term past performance and fundamental structures that will provide a solid foundation for growth. Management is a big part of that, and a big part of management is not only how efficiently a company produces a product or how innovative an offering is, but how effectively its management structure invests money to create return.

ROIC, as defined by Warren Buffett, Morningstar, and others, is a calculation in which a company's net operating profit is considered as a function of its invested capital. Pat Dorsey describes the value of ROIC this way:

> Finally, there's return on invested capital (ROIC), which combines the best of both worlds. It measures the return on all capital invested in the firm, regardless of whether it is equity or debt. So, it incorporates debt—unlike

ROA—but removes the distortion that can make highly leveraged companies look very profitable using ROE. It also uses a different definition of profits that helps remove any effects caused by a company's financing decisions (debt versus equity), so we can get as close as possible to a number that represents the true efficiency of the underlying business. There are a number of ways to calculate ROIC, and the formula can be complicated, so it is not a readily available number like ROA and ROE. The upshot is that you should interpret ROIC the same way as ROE and ROA—a higher return is preferable to a lower one.[2]

The equation looks like this:

Net Operating Profit after Taxes (NOPAT)/ Invested Capital (IC) = ROIC

Why is this a good measurement of the quality of management? Well, because it shows foresight and restraint, good decision making, and a keen understanding that a company that spends its money well does so to generate more money. It is also another indicator of a strong competitive moat. Those companies that invest their money well are able to stay ahead of the competition. They are able to make investments that protect their positions, keeping them in front or isolated from others.

It's important to note that ROIC is not the same as a company's return on equity (ROE). ROE is a measurement of profitability that calculates the amount of profit a company generates with money shareholders have invested.[3] That equation looks like this:

ROE = Net Income/Shareholder's Equity

---

[2] Pat Dorsey, *The Little Book that Builds Wealth* (Hoboken, NJ: Wiley, 2008).
[3] See www.investopedia.com/terms/r/returnonequity.asp.

ROIC, while far from perfect, is a much better indicator of good management than the simple ROE calculation. That's why I prefer it when making decisions for the 52-Week Low strategy. By this point in the strategy process, we've already identified companies with strong economics that allow for wide competitive moats. We've also identified companies that are worth taking the risk of investing in through their free cash flow yield calculations. ROIC helps us to understand not just the industry and the investing landscape but the fundamental soundness of individual companies.

Warren Buffett, in his 1992 letter to shareholders, codified the importance of ROIC this way:

> Leaving the question of price aside, the best business to own is one that over an extended period can employ large amounts of incremental capital at very high rates of return. The worst business to own is one that must, or will, do the opposite—that is, consistently employ ever-greater amounts of capital at very low rates of return.

Buffett reinforced his position on the importance of ROIC at the 1998 Berkshire Hathaway Annual Meeting, when he put it this way: "If you have a business that's earning 20 percent to 25 percent on equity, time is your friend. But time is your enemy if your money is in a low-return business."

Essentially, he's saying that the companies that create the most value over the long haul are the ones that can invest large amounts of incremental capital to create proportionately—or disproportionately—large returns. Companies with low ROIC tend to invest even more while making less.

It's relatively straightforward in concept, but ROIC reveals a lot more than simple financial performance. It is an indication of management consistency and good decision making. But it's important that ROIC is looked at as a trend, not as a single-year metric, in order to provide insight into how a company will perform in the future. In this regard, it is a judgment tool, a way of sizing up a company mathematically for often unquantifiable traits, like strategy and intelligence of leadership.

A Complicated Measurement

There are complications when determining a company's ROIC, though. It's not a simple calculation, and there is a lot of judgment that goes into even understanding the measurements that it is made up of. For one thing, you can't simply take a snapshot of a month, a quarter, or a year and understand how well the management invests capital. I look at each company's ROIC over a 10-year period to ensure that management has been quite effective in earning returns north of their cost of capital.

Second, the reporting needed to determine ROIC is not standard. You can't simply look at the balance sheet to get a sense of it. There's art involved with the science of ROIC. You have to make judgments, which we will get into a little later, but for now, let's take a closer look at the equation used to determine ROIC:

$$ROIC = (NOPAT)/(IC)$$

Because NOPAT and IC are both nonstandard measurements, it can be difficult to calculate. This is where the judgment calls come in. NOPAT, the numerator, is fairly straightforward. But it's worth a closer look.

Morningstar explains it this way as part of its educational materials:[4]

> Notice the numerator is a nonstandard measure, meaning you will not find it on any standard financial statement. We have to calculate it ourselves. The name "net operating

---

[4]See http://news.morningstar.com/classroom2/course.asp?docId=145095&page=9.

profit, after taxes" is fairly descriptive, but you can also think about NOPAT as simply net income with interest expense (net of taxes) added back. We do this to figure out what the profit would be without taking a company's capital structure into consideration.

NOPAT = (Operating Profit) × (1 − Tax Rate)

You won't find IC on a financial statement either. In part, this is because narrowing down capital expenditures and determining which are investments and which are simply the costs of doing business is, in itself, a somewhat tricky business. Again, from Morningstar:

> For the denominator, invested capital is yet another non-standard, calculated measure not found on any financial statement. Invested capital tries to measure exactly how much capital is required to operate a business. It can be defined as such:

IC = (Total Assets) − (Excess Cash)
− (Non-Interest-Bearing Current Liabilities)

They go on to list examples of "non-interest-bearing current liabilities" like accounts payable. Money spent is not money invested. Paying bills is not an investment, it is an obligation that will not make more money. Deferred revenues and deferred taxes are also examples, though there is a lot of judgment that goes into determining what is invested capital and what is simply an expenditure.

What we hope to determine is the strength of a company's ROIC. Strong ROIC—in excess of 15 percent, according to Morningstar, over a number of years and clearly exceeding the cost of capital—indicates a strong moat in the form of good management. Despite popular excitement, this kind of good management is often a sign of maturity rather than fame. Weak ROIC—that below Morningstar's 15 percent threshold or that below the cost of capital—is an indication of one of a few things:

- Unstable management.
- A weak economic moat (poor competitive advantages that make it difficult for a company to maintain long-term growth).
- Debt that is eroding return.

Understanding the calculations and the decisions that go into ROIC, let's take a look at how using ROIC can help identify opportunities where other investors may not think to look and why it's important to look at ROIC over the long term.

Turning Back the Clock

Let's go back to 2008, the year of the market implosion. It was a time of great uncertainty. I probably don't need to remind you (and I apologize for the ulcer-inducing memory) that the market was something that can be underdescribed as volatile in those days. Any given day was bringing three-digit swings in the Dow and it seemed that America's economic ship was being tossed and thrown by the storm surrounding the market and years from ever being righted.

This was a time of both great peril and opportunity for investors. The trouble was being able to distinguish between the two. Two of the Big Three automakers were still reeling from having to drive to Congress hat in hand, and the mortgage market was in shambles. Bailouts and fiscal policy were hot-button political fodder. And yet, amid all this uncertainty, there were a few companies that stood out, stood above in terms of popular opinion: Apple, Amazon, and Google, just to name a few.

In some circles, Silicon Valley seemed to be the last bastion of hope. And perhaps the brightest star among the shimmering galaxy was Google. It seemed the search giant was capable of anything. Google is so entrenched in the lead when it comes to search, it is easy to forget that the company did not invent the practice. Far from it.

In fact, prior to Google's ascension, another oddly named search company had the world captivated. Yahoo! was once synonymous with search. Long before Google's initial public offering (IPO), Yahoo! had investors seeing the possibility in search.

Now, it should be pointed out that not all search is the same. Search engines operate on algorithms that connect search terms to possible matches in files that exist on massive server farms around the world. In a fraction of a second, these files are indexed, and recommendations are made based on relevance to the original query. Some algorithms are better than others. Some technology is better at that indexing than others. But this is not the story of technology; it is a story about management.

Both Google and Yahoo! are in the same business. They make access to information via the Internet easy. But their stories, particularly when viewed through the lens of ROIC, could not be more different.

Let's start with Yahoo! When the company went public in 1998, its ROIC was predictably low. Many companies, when they are getting up and running, have a hard time delivering ROIC because their models haven't matured and they are not generating return. So, in 1998, according to SeekingAlpha.com,[5] the company's ROIC was negative. They were losing money on the money they invested.

---

[5] "Using ROIC to Find Stocks with Great Management," Seeking Alpha, (*The Curious Investor* blog), February 10, 2009, http://seekingalpha.com/article/119602-using-roic -to-find-stocks-with-great-management-autozone-yahoo-google.

This, in and of itself, is not all that concerning. What is concerning is that the trend never really reverses and that has as much to do with Yahoo!'s management as anything else.

Yahoo's IPO happened before it was truly profitable and was very much still in its growth phase. Furthermore, Yahoo quickly embarked on a course as an industry consolidator using its balance sheet to acquire new businesses in hopes of creating scale. Because the ROIC equation used relies on TTM net income versus debt and equity capital on the balance sheet at the end of a period, this measure is necessarily backward looking. Thus, for any earlier stage growth company, we'd expect to see initially low ROIC but an eventual rise as invested capital begins generating return. However, the problem is that Yahoo is unable to maintain ROIC anywhere above 10 percent on a sustained basis. Given that there are many attractive equity opportunities that return 10+ percent, it is hard to imagine why investors would want to keep their money invested at Yahoo, which is continually reinvesting net income at such a low return.

In fact, according to the same Seeking Alpha case study, Yahoo!'s ROIC peaked in 2005 at 20 percent but, in the decade between its IPO and the 2008 report, only managed to top 10 percent twice.

Google, however, took a completely different approach. The company waited until 2002, when it was already profitable, to do its IPO. It didn't suffer from the sluggish start of other new companies. Its ROIC in 2002 was nearly 55 percent. Again, you probably want to ignore early figures and focus on trends. But Google's worst year between 2002 and 2008 delivered a higher ROIC than Yahoo!'s second-best year. In 2004, the ROIC fell expectedly, as Google put significant capital on its books, a remnant of its IPO. It has maintained an average ROIC over 15 percent to 18 percent for most of its existence.

These ROIC figures serve as canaries in the coal mine as it relates to stock price, much as they did with respect to WorldCom and Enron. Again, from Seeking Alpha:

> Between 1998 and 2008, Yahoo's stock shows an initial flurry of interest in the stock due to much investor exuberance over the company's potential for outsized growth. This exuberance collapses as Yahoo finds itself unable to realize ROIC in excess of 5 percent over its first four years as a public company. While the company's efforts seem to begin returning positively between 2003 and 2005, it is short lived and a history of poor acquisitions and investments in poorly timed strategic initiatives take its toll. From 2003–2008, just as you'd expect from a business with a long run ROIC below its cost of capital the stock has simply tread water. Yahoo would have done better by shareholders by distributing annual income and allowing shareholders to reallocate to other investments.

Yahoo!'s management has made poor decisions time and time again, wagering on bets that simply didn't pay off. They weren't able to deliver real value to shareholders, and it has left a once-promising Internet giant treading water.

Look at that last sentence again: "Yahoo would have done better by shareholders by distributing annual income and allowing shareholders to reallocate to other investments."

Essentially, that's saying that management should not be trusted to invest capital on behalf of shareholders and instead should return the money so investors can make better decisions. That's a tough pill for any company to swallow and stands in stark contrast to Google's stock performance, which has trended positive since nearly day one.

Management has also shown an ability to deliver 15–18 percent ROIC every year since receiving IPO dollars, as with all retained earnings from the business. Google, like Yahoo, has never paid a dividend and thus shareholders have chosen to entrust management with re-investing profits. Google, however, has delivered and valuation has increased at an annualized 31 percent since inception. It's interesting to note, however, that valuation has expanded faster than the business has generated return on its invested capital. Might this be a worrisome sign? In both the Yahoo and Google cases, we've seen that stock appreciation tends to lead and over shoot steady state ROIC, but we've also seen that the market generally corrects itself as expectations become more reasonable.

Google's proven ability to generate positive ROIC year after year has created a rise in stock price. That rise in stock price is reflective of investor confidence that the company will make good decisions. Greater confidence, greater stock price, greater return—these are all things that have allowed Google to widen the competitive moat between it and Yahoo!. More money means more innovation, more refinement of its offerings, and the freedom and material resources to explore new programs and revenue streams.

If you were investing in 2006 and looked at ROIC only for 2005, you would have seen Yahoo! at 20 percent and Google at 15 percent and thought Yahoo! was the better bet. You would have been wrong. Yahoo!'s ROIC in 2006 fell to just over 5 percent and continued to drop the next two years. This illustrates the importance of looking at trends.

ROIC is a measurement of collective good decisions. You generate positive ROIC over the course of time, not in a flash. Good management is about consistency, not fame. And that consistency is what distinguishes a good, well-run company that is undervalued from a famous one that underperforms.

In his updated white paper for the *Harvard Business Review*, Michael Porter succinctly describes the value of ROIC when measuring a company's performance.

> Return on sales or the growth rate of profits fail to account for the capital required to compete in the industry," Porter writes. "We utilize earnings before interest and taxes divided by average invested capital less cash as the measure of ROIC. This measure controls for idiosyncratic differences in capital structure and tax rates across companies and industries.[6]

In other words, ROIC doesn't lie. While behemoths like WorldCom and Enron had investors fooled by their high stock prices, the ROIC of the two firms revealed warning signs of the truth that would eventually devastate the market, wipe out people's savings, and leave a lasting scar on the investing world. ROIC is the story of a company's real value. Not the cover story of magazines, not the alluring tale of rising stock prices, but the real story of a company's ability to make good investment decisions that yield long-term value.

Combining ROIC with the other four filters of the 52-Week Low help us to follow the legendary Warren Buffett's rule number 1 of investing: Never lose money. The second rule? Never forget rule number 1. In order to do so, we need to separate potential investments in two groups: those that increase the risk of breaking rule number 1 and those that stand the best chance of decreasing it. That's what the 52-Week Low is designed to do, and understanding ROIC is a big—though certainly not the only—part of making those considered decisions.

---

[6]Michael Porter, "The Five Competitive Forces That Shape Strategy," *Harvard Business Review,* January 2008.

CHAPTER 8

This Time Is Never Different

Jacobian Inverse: I want to believe that the risks and returns embedded in today's markets look nothing like anything in the past. There is always something new under the sun, and it is hopeless to study the past to help me make informed present-time decisions.

Maybe this seems absurd, but, unfortunately, many investors behave as if what is happening within the markets is completely new and unprecedented when, in fact, if you study financial history, you will find many common threads between the past bubbles and bursts.

In a March 2011 GMO white paper, James Montier presented his "Seven Immutable Laws of Investing." These seven principles, when taken as a whole, provide a nice basis for investing behavior that should lead to long-term gains and include:

1. Always insist on a margin of safety.
2. This time is never different.
3. Be patient and wait for the fat pitch.
4. Be contrarian.
5. Risk is the permanent loss of capital, never a number.
6. Be leery of leverage.
7. Never invest in something you don't understand.

Pretty good advice, but the one that stood out was the second one: this time is never different. Montier quotes Sir John Templeton, who says "this time is different" are the four most dangerous words in investment. I believe he's right. You don't have to look too far back in history to know that it repeats itself, that markets become inflated and bubbles swell until they burst. The idea that a new bubble is somehow different than the old ones because it looks a little different is ludicrous. History repeats itself for good and for bad.

After all, how different was the real estate bubble and burst from the dot-com bubble? In both cases, investors were not behaving rationally but were rationalizing, buying dot-com stocks with no earnings. Real estate prices were increasing at astronomical rates as the conventional wisdom was: "It is different this time in real estate. God only made a certain amount of land in the world, and after all, with land you can feel it, touch it, live on it, and build on it." That is a true statement on all the uses of land, but what could not be explained rationally was the surge and irrational exuberance around the momentum of real estate prices.

When the world was going gaga over the Internet bubble or the prices of California real estate were tripling every year, we should have known what was going to come next. We should have seen it coming, but most of us didn't. Or, if we did, we refused to acknowledge it. But bubbles and bursts are only one way of looking at the idea that "this time is never different." The negative way. There's a positive comfort that comes from knowing that history is bound to repeat itself, which can be seen only by those with the discipline to look for it. That positive, as I see it, can be defined in a single word: value.

Value, like bubbles, never changes. Value and value-based investment strategies are like the tortoises in the fabled race, and bubbles are the hare. Value investing means identifying undervalued and overlooked companies and investing in them for a finite amount of time, then selling and repeating the process. You may never make overnight billions, but you should not lose them either. You should make consistent returns over the long haul. When the bubble has burst and is sleeping by the side of the road, you'll pass by and win the race.

During the dot-com bubble, when companies with no intrinsic or inherent value were skyrocketing in price like a hare out of the starting gates, people like Warren Buffett were pacing themselves with value investments. Even as the crowd and media were heralding in a new age of prosperity and declaring value dead, value investors marched along at a steady pace, leaving the hares in their tracks when the bubble burst.

So while Templeton and Montier may view the phrase "this time is never different" as a warning, I prefer to think of it as reassuring opportunity. This time is never different. Value never changes, and those tortoises with the discipline to stick to value should always win the race.

"Simply hoping that bad things won't happen again is not an investment strategy," Montier quotes Templeton.[1] "Pay attention to mistakes and learn from them."

In 1999, Warren Buffett lost it. Or, at least that's what newspapers and magazines were saying about him. Berkshire Hathaway had reported small net increases per share for investors and had avoided the dot-com boom. Up and comers, hot shots, and day traders were proclaiming the changing of the guard. Gone was Buffett's old guard approach to investing. Here was the high-tech, fast-moving, constantly shifting market of the digital age.

How did Buffett respond? In the 2000 letter to Berkshire Hathaway shareholders,[2] he had this to say:

> The line separating investment and speculation, which is never bright and clear, becomes blurred still further

---

[1] See Bob Parkman, "Consider These Words of Wisdom about Investing," September 20, 2006, www.sirjohntempleton.org/articles_details.asp?a=16.
[2] Available at www.berkshirehathaway.com/2000ar/2000letter.html.

when most market participants have recently enjoyed triumphs. Nothing sedates rationality like large doses of effortless money. After a heady experience of that kind, normally sensible people drift into behavior akin to that of Cinderella at the ball. They know that overstaying the festivities—that is, continuing to speculate in companies that have gigantic valuations relative to the cash they are likely to generate in the future—will eventually bring on pumpkins and mice. But they nevertheless hate to miss a single minute of what is one helluva party. Therefore, the giddy participants all plan to leave just seconds before midnight. There's a problem, though: They are dancing in a room in which the clocks have no hands.

And, in 2001, after the collapse, once it was proved that his skepticism of huge earnings without corresponding value was correct, he told the world he told them so.[3] The fact is, an investor who takes the route devoted to intrinsic value and patience will often find him or herself on the right side of hindsight. Bubbles will always build and burst. There will always be a new and improved way of doing things. There will always be a time when the tried and true devotion to intrinsic value will be called outdated and out of touch. The key is to train your ear to recognize the rhyme of history as it is echoing and turn the eventual burst into your biggest opportunity.

Or, as Buffett once said, "Look at market fluctuations as your friend rather than your enemy; profit from folly rather than participate in it."

---

[3] "Warren Buffett: 'I Told You So,'" *BBC News*, March 13, 2001, http://news.bbc.co .uk/2/hi/business/1217716.stm.

CHAPTER 9

Filter 4: Long-Term Debt to Free Cash Flow Ratio

Jacobian Inverse: I want to find businesses that, when an economic setback occurs, would have a challenging time staying competitive, let alone staying in business. After all, leverage can help magnify business results in the good times, and I would prefer to not think about what could happen in the bad times.

Extreme thinking helps me realize that I need to be mindful of a business's balance sheet because it not a question of *will* an economic setback happen but *when*. Economic setbacks are inevitable for any business. Leverage can magnify business results for the good and for the bad. I am most concerned about planning for the bad.

Bruce Berkowitz does his best to kill a company before he buys it. It is this process that helps Bruce identify all the various economic setbacks that should they happen could the business in question survive.

"We look at companies, count the cash, and then try to kill the company," he writes. "We spend a lot of time thinking about what could go wrong with a company . . . We try every which way to kill our best ideas. If we can't kill it, maybe we're on to something."[1]

It's the oldest advice in personal finance and it takes many forms: Save for a rainy day. Prepare for the worst and hope for the best. Don't buy things you can't afford. Live within your means.

It's good advice, too. And not just because your father or grandmother gave it to you. It's good advice because it reveals a fundamental fact of life and money: Bad times will happen and you have to be prepared. You may lose your job or get hurt and need to take a leave of absence. There are all kinds of reasons to pad your savings with enough cash to make sure you can cover your bills, your mortgage, your living expenses in case something should happen.

Savings are important, but so is understanding the relationship between the money you make (salary, for example) and the amount of debt you take on to build your lifestyle. You don't have to look too far into the past to see the damage done when this relationship is ignored. The mortgage crisis of 2008 was the direct result of people overleveraging themselves and ending up in hot water. With little savings and not enough revenue to cover the monthly mortgage, Americans were losing their homes by the hundreds of thousands, and an already delicate system of lending and borrowing was thrown into turmoil. The effects were felt for years.

This is Personal Finance 101 stuff, the lessons we should all have learned in high school. But the principles that should guide our personal financial decisions are the same ones that differentiate good companies that provide downside protection from those flash-in-the-pan companies with rapid growth and, usually, ultimate decline.

A company's long-term debt to free cash flow ratio is an indication of its ability to survive and thrive during a downturn.

---

[1] Quoted in "Kill the Company," from James Montier's *The Little Book of Behavioral Investing* (Hoboken, NJ: Wiley, 2010).

Highly leveraged companies—those with long-term debt that greatly exceeds several years of their annual free cash flow—will find it crippling to service its debts during downturns. This second kind of company seems, on the surface, to be the kind most logical investors would avoid, but do they?

A 2004 GMO white paper titled "The Case for Quality—The Danger of Junk" compares the way investors make decisions as it relates to highly leveraged companies to a trip to a casino or the purchase of a lottery ticket:

> Rational investors should demand higher returns whenever higher risk is assumed. And, while this relationship generally holds true at the asset class level, rather astonishingly, it completely breaks down at the stock level. In fact, it appears that investors *overpay* for higher risk stocks and *underpay* for less risky stocks. This pattern of high return for low risk exists both in small and large caps and in global equity markets alike.
>
> A quick glance at the world around us provides ample circumstantial evidence as to why investors might overpay for risky stocks. For example, if people are risk-averse, why do casinos exist and how do lottery tickets sell? In both of these cases the expected return on "investment" is negative, yet business for both is booming.[2]

Why does this happen? Why do rational people go to casinos or buy lottery tickets? Well, the simple answer is that rationality has nothing to do with it. It is the curse of the big win. Deep down, many of us believe we are going to be the one, the special one who has the winning ticket or wins the big jackpot. You can tell us the odds all you want, remind us that it is statistically more likely that you will be struck by lightning than that you will win the lottery, but that type of reason

---

[2]GMO, "The Case for Quality—The Danger of Junk," white paper, March 2004.

seems to pale in comparison to the sheer size of the lottery jackpot on the sign above the kiosk where you buy tickets.

But the lottery and casinos have one built-in precautionary factor that protects those of us who eschew reason and buy in: at least in these situations, everyone is, theoretically, paying the same price to play. Lottery tickets don't get more expensive the more people play. Antes and minimum table bets are the same no matter how many people are sitting at the table. When you take a risk in the market, this is not the case. When those with big eyes for big prizes begin buying stocks, prices rise and become overinflated. Next thing you know, there is a herd of people all paying increasingly exorbitant prices for overvalued long shots.

And all of this can be avoided by simply using logic and rules to guide your investment choices. Look at the odds of the lottery win and walk away. Look at the size of the Vegas casinos and understand that these massive structures were not built by winners and choose, instead, to go see a show. Have a process in place for identifying good companies that are not overleveraged and avoid the crowds, underpaying for less risky stocks.

This is what the fourth filter of the 52-Week Low formula helps us do: Apply logic to identifying the companies that are prepared for downturns and avoid those that are less likely to survive and thrive in times of recovery.

When it comes to debt, I'm hawkish. Warren Buffett, who once again appears as an influential thought leader in this book, looks at a company's long-term debt-to-net-earnings ratio from the viewpoint of an owner. If he were to purchase the company outright, assuming all its cash, earnings, and debt, he wants to see that the company could pay off all of its long-term obligations with cash and current earnings (no growth) in five years or less.[3] This five-year threshold is also

---

[3] Darryl Daté-Shappard, "3 Things Warren Buffett Looks for in a Company before Buying," *The Motley Fool*, October 22, 2013, www.fool.com.au/2013/10/22/3-things-warren-buffett-looks-for-in-a-company-before-buying/.

referenced in the book *The New Buffettology*, by Mary Buffett and David Clarke, in the chapter titled, "Warren's Checklist for Potential Investments: His Ten Points of Light," where it states: "Companies with a durable competitive advantage typically have long-term debt burdens of fewer than five times current net earnings." I'm more aggressive than that, preferring instead to see a ratio of no more than 3, meaning that a company has the ability to pay off its long-term debts in no more than three years.

Why? Because I can be. I take an owner's view of a company that I'm considering investing in, but I don't behave like an owner. Because I'm not actually buying companies outright, I can take a short-term view. The list of 25 companies in the 52-Week Low formula is reviewed every six months, which means I can focus on the short-term impact of long-term debt. I want to be assured that a company that I am about to purchase, though the stock price is down and Wall Street's enthusiasm is low, has a balance sheet that is iron clad, and it is able to maintain and grow operations based on existing free cash flow for the next sixth months. I am thus more aggressive in avoiding long-term leverage than even Buffett.

This helps to ensure we are not buying a company whose price is low and is riddled with debt because that business might continue to reach lower and lower values. This helps keep me from investing in what's called a *value trap* or *catching a falling knife*, which means you run a high probability of permanent loss of capital.[4]

Unlike other metrics I've pointed out in this book, which required us to take a long, multiyear look at free cash flow yield and return on invested capital (ROIC), the long-term debt to free cash flow ratio is one I want to look at in a snapshot, the last reporting cycle. I'm less concerned with how much debt a company has carried over the years than I am with how much it has right now. If a company makes it to this

---

[4]Steven Petty, "Value Traps and Investor Psychology," *American Century Investments* blog, December 20, 2011, http://americancenturyblog.com/2011/12/value-traps-and-investor-psychology/.

filter, we already know there is a high probability it has a durable competitive advantage, free cash flow yield with a margin of safety, and a knack for building shareholder value growth, as demonstrated by consistent ROIC above its cost of capital.

We understand the trends, so we can begin looking at the opportunity.

Calculating Long-Term Debt to Free Cash Flow

Unlike the calculations that go into determining the ROIC, which require a certain amount of conjecture and thought, calculating a company's debt positioning is pretty simple.

The equation looks like this:

(Total Long-Term Debt)/Free Cash Flow

What the answer to this equation will tell us is how long it will take a company, assuming free cash flow remains constant, to pay off its existing debt. The lower the number, the better.

Let's look at how this works, once again using ice cream trucks.

Truck A is owned by Gary. Gary has been in business for nearly a decade. He made some capital improvements to his truck, and, in order to do so, he recently took on $3,000 in debt in the form of a loan from the bank. Revenues have been pretty solid, and his free cash flow (FCF) is $1,500.

Truck B is owned by Sam. Sam is relatively new to the business. As such, he has had to buy a lot—truck, ice cream, serving utensils, and cones. He has a business loan of $35,000. Sam's also pretty good at public relations and is making some fancy ice cream. He does a lot of volume and is doing a nice job of keeping his operating expenses down. His FCF is $3,000—twice that of Gary's FCF.

Gary's truck is small and established. Sam's is the hottest thing in town. But how do they stack up? Let's do the math.

Truck A (Gary)

Long-term debt: $3,000

FCF: $1,500

$$\frac{\$3,000 \ (debt)}{\$1,500 \ (FCF)} = 2 \ years$$

Gary would be able to pay off his debt in 24 months.

Truck B (Sam)

Long-term debt: $35,000

FCF: $3,000

$$\frac{\$35,000 \ (debt)}{\$3,000 \ (FCF)} = 11.66 \ years$$

Sam would be able to pay off his debt in 140 months.

Sam's truck may be positioning itself for greater long-term value by creating a clear point of differentiation from a business modeling perspective, but as investors and believers in the 52-Week Low formula, we are not trying to discover visionaries. We are trying to identify valuable investments. Being hawkish when it comes to debt helps to protect our investments against short-term catastrophic failure.

You may believe the preceding example is not found in the real world. As you will see soon within this chapter, there are many situations whereby two seemingly equal competitors are far from equal when it comes to their debt situation.

A Few Notes about Debt

This chapter may give a reader the impression that I'm against debt, and I suppose I am somewhat. A lot of debt concerns me when it comes to making intelligent choices about investing. But there is a distinction between how I view debt as an investor and how a CEO may view debt as it relates to his company.

Debt is a fact of life and a fact of business. And, as such, it can be both positive and negative. Positive debt—your mortgage, for instance—is a sign of investment in the future. Other debt, like credit cards used to buy a cup of coffee and left to fester, gathering interest, is negative.

The same goes with business. If a company takes on debt to expand its manufacturing capacity or to modernize its data security, that in and of itself is, a very good thing. If a company takes on debt just to keep the lights on, take notice and turn the other way.

If you are an officer or employee of a company that takes on the former, it may give you a solid reason to believe that the company is positioning itself for greatness and expansion. If you work for the latter, sharpen up your resume.

But this book is not about how to think and behave like an employee of a company because you are not. You don't work for the companies in which you invest, so you cannot respond or consider issues as an employee might. You cannot be inspired by the visionary leadership of a CEO. You cannot take into account the game-changing innovation in the pipeline. You cannot be a fan or an emotional critic. You must be disinterested and data-centric.

The sociologist Abraham Maslow—of Maslow's Hierarchy of Needs fame—described the way we choose to respond to information or situations by saying that between stimulus and response, there is space. That space is the place where we consider the stimulus and formulate a response strategy. In our earliest days, that space was very small. We responded by instinct, usually one of the three "Fs"—fight, flight, or freeze—as in:

Stimulus: A saber-toothed tiger is chasing you.

Space: None

Response: Run

But modernity has widened that space for consideration, yet too often we don't take advantage of it. We act by instinct or out of emotion, rather than logic. Investing is a place where we need to have guides and structures in place to ensure that we use the space well. In other words, we need filters and processes in mind in order to avoid the "yeah, but" response to things like debt, as in:

Stimulus: The company has taken on $2 billion in debt to support capital investments, which looks bad.

Space: I believe in my gut in this CEO.

Response: Yeah, but they are doing it to cure cancer, so I'll take the risk.

The 52-Week Low formula is about eliminating the instinct to believe or feel when it comes to investing and replace it with sound logic that is dispassionate. Emotions, feelings, and, perhaps worst of all, inspiration clouds our judgment. It weakens our logical resolve.

There are a lot of inspiring or famous or familiar companies out there. Some of them may be right for the formula; some may not be. Still others may not be right now, but someday. Don't allow inspiration to cloud your judgment. Invest for value and results. If you need to be inspired, find a company or CEO you believe in and try to get a job.

Of all the filters subject to inspiration clouding, this fourth one is the most vulnerable, because debt seems to be easily justifiable. Don't justify. Stick to your process, stick to the program. Use that space between stimulus and response to remember to think like an investor, not an employee or admirer.

Long-Term Debt to Free Cash Flow: Head-to-Head

To show how companies within the same industry—indeed, companies with nearly identical business models, offerings, and consumer awareness—compare to one another, the following section is about head-to-head match-ups. One company is in a much better position from a long-term debt to free cash flow perspective. Do think you'll be able to tell which one? How? Stock price? Familiarity? You might be surprised.

Using snapshots of free cash flow and long-term debt from December 2013,[5] I hope the following comparisons illustrate the importance of doing your homework when evaluating a company's financial health and how the data can be quite different among direct competitors and across two very disparate industries: heavy equipment and cosmetics.

Bout 1: Heavy Equipment

Cummins versus Caterpillar Cummins Inc. (CMI) and Caterpillar Inc. (CAT) are both in the business of making really big, powerful motorized things. If you've spent any time driving through construction zones or near building sites, chances are good you've seen their products. Caterpillar products in their distinctive yellow and black paint. Cummins may come barreling up to you in your rearview mirror on the vent badge of a semi Ram pick-up truck.

Popularly, Caterpillar is the more familiar name, but Cummins certainly is well known among those who care about such things. And, based on these, you might expect Caterpillar to have less in the way of long-term debt or burden. Remember back to earlier chapters about the fear of missing out. Fame, like it or not, does have an impact on the market. But this is a case where familiarity is wrong. Here's how the companies stack up.

Caterpillar is a much larger company from a revenue perspective, but there are a lot of things that can influence stock valuation. Here's how they stack up in terms of trailing 12 months (TTM) of revenue and FCF.

---

[5]From S&P Capital IQ as of December 12, 2013.

Revenues TTM

Cummins: $17.005 billion
Caterpillar: $57.32 billion

FCF TTM

Cummins: $1.395 billion
Caterpillar: $4.921 billion

Caterpillar is over three times the size of Cummins when it comes to revenue and FCF.

Which company do you believe is better positioned from a debt perspective? Both make similar equipment and, presumably, require similar capital investments for manufacturing. They have similar ratios of revenue to FCF. But Caterpillar brings in so much more revenue. It has to be the one I would invest in, right?

Wrong. Look at total long-term debt and you'll see why.

Long-Term Debt

Cummins: $1.731 billion
Caterpillar: $26.015 billion

That is a stark contrast. Let's do the calculations:

Cummins: $1.731 billion (debt) divided by $1.395 billion (FCF) = 1.24 years or in less than 15 months. So, should Cummins decide to, they could pay off all of their long-term debt in a short-term period.

Caterpillar: $26.015 billion (debt) divided by $4.921 billion (FCF) = 5.29 years. So, should Caterpillar decide to pay off all of their long-term debt, it would take more than five years to do so.

Cummins is in a much better position to manage in and thrive through an economic downturn.

Bout 2: Cosmetics

L'Oreal versus Revlon   As an industry, cosmetics is huge. Profit margins tend to outpace other consumer packaged goods because of the perception of high switching costs among consumers, which results from huge amounts of brand loyalty. Try to convince a woman to change cosmetics brands, and you'll see what I mean. And for decades, L'Oreal SA (LRLCY) and Revlon, Inc. (REV) have been ubiquitous and popular mainstays in the global beauty industry.

L'Oreal is a true industry leader, with more than $22.98 billion in revenue and a market cap valuation of $104.25 billion in December 2013. Revlon, a popular brand in and of itself, is a clear second fiddle, with a fraction of the revenue and 1 percent of the market cap valuation.

Are you forming any conclusions? The Cummins-Caterpillar example showed that having bigger revenues doesn't mean you have better debt positioning. Does that mean Revlon is actually in better shape than L'Oreal? Let's see.

FCF TTM

L'Oreal: $3.57 billion
Revlon: $68 million

Now, if this example followed the Cummins-Caterpillar example, we would look at total debt and discover that L'Oreal is significantly more leveraged than Revlon, that it's total debt exceeds total cash, and that Revlon has comparatively little debt. Does it follow the same pattern?

Long-Term Debt

L'Oreal: $56.4 million

Revlon: $1.228 billion

The calculations:

L'Oreal: $56.4 million (debt) divided by $3.57 billion (FCF) = 0.016 years or in less than 6 days. So if L'Oreal wanted to pay-off their long-term debt, they could do so in less than a week.

Revlon: $1.228 billion (debt) divided by $68 million (FCF) = 18.05 years. So, if Revlon wanted to pay-off their long-term debt, it would take them just over 18 years to do so.

L'Oreal is clearly in a better position, thanks to its free cash flow and comparatively little debt. This case shows us that just because one company is David and the other is Goliath, Goliath does not always lose (Table 9.1).

Table 9.1   Other Examples of Free Cash Flow to Long-Term Debt Comparisons among Competing Companies*

52-Week Low Fourth Filter Winners		52-Week Low Fourth Filter Losers	
< 3 years		> 3 years	
Walgreens	1.45 years	Rite Aid	14.49 years
Cummins Engines	1.24 years	Deere & Company	24.55 years
Ritchie Brothers	2.85 years	Caterpillar	5.29 years
General Mills	2.66 years	Copart	14.79 years
Illinois Tool Works	1.85 years	ConAgra	12.37 years
Schlumberger Ltd.	2.06 years	General Electric	20.66 years
Disney	1.96 years	Baker Hughes	5 years
Advance Auto		Time Warner	5.55 years
Parts	1.67 years	AutoZone	4.48 years
L'Oreal	6 days	Revlon	18.06 years
Union Pacific	2.76 years	Norfolk Southern	10.74 years

*From S&P Capital IQ as of December 12, 2013.

Summing It Up

Understanding a company's debt position and having rigid rules in place about how much debt is acceptable is vital to protecting your short-term investment and maximizing value potential. Just like you were told to save for a rainy day when you were young, companies and industries don't always know when the weather is going to get bad, and the better prepared and positioned they are, the more likely they are to be able to weather whatever comes their way.

Think like an investor, not an employee or admirer. Don't allow inspiration or admiration—or disdain or fear—to allow you to justify investing in a company that lacks a specific amount of long-term coverage with free cash flow. Remember to be hawkish because, as an investor, you can be. And, ultimately, because being hawkish on debt should protect your investment.

Case Study: Don't Believe the Hype When It Comes to Value

Jacobian Inverse: If I want to ensure that I minimize my potential gains and limit growth in my investments, I will seek only companies that are already popular among the media and buyers. I will seek herds. I will avoid companies with more sellers than buyers to all but guarantee that I overpay for overvalued stocks. I will be sure to avoid all companies with negative popular sentiment and focus only on those companies that everyone—from Wall Street to Main Street—is in love with.

Of all the people that have shaped my approach to investing, Howard Marks is among the most important, and his thoughts, specifically around the influence of trends and social biases that impact investing, are important, especially if you want to do better than the status quo.

Marks wrote:

There's only one way to describe most investors: trend followers. Superior investors are the exact opposite. Superior investing, as I hope I've convinced you by now, requires second-level thinking—a way of thinking that's different from that of others, more complex and more insightful. By definition, most of the crowd can't share it. Thus, the judgments of the crowd can't hold the key to success. Rather, the trend, the consensus view, is something to game against, and the consensus portfolio is one to diverge from. As the pendulum swings or the market goes through its cycles, the key to ultimate success lies in doing the opposite.*

When you adopt a value strategy like the 52-Week Low, there are a few things you need to become comfortable with quickly. Comfort in these areas will help you to identify value opportunities and will also help to keep you away from the market crowds that drive prices up. Those things you must get comfortable with are (in no particular order):

- *Data is a decision-making tool, not sentiment or gut feelings.* It's hard for a company to hide from its reporting. Sometimes this means you will walk away from a quantitatively unstable company with positive popular and market sentiment. Other times, it will be the thing that helps you understand the real value of a company when sentiment has turned.
- *Trailing losses are or can be a good thing.* I'll cover this in more detail in another case study, but outperforming the market means looking where others aren't, and most people turn away when performance has been bad. A value investor picks apart the carcass of an abandoned stock looking for signs of life that others have overlooked. They get excited to do this because finding signs of life and structural integrity is how we find value.
- *You are an investor, not a consumer.* Consumers make decisions based on opinion—theirs, their friends', the prevailing wisdom of the neighborhood. For a consumer, the sample size is small, limited usually to your circle of friends or the culture in which you live. It's easy to forget that consumers have only a small idea of the real value of a company in the marketplace. Investors look for intrinsic value, not lifestyle relevance.

I highlight these three things at the beginning of this section as a prelude to what follows. Here, I want to share three examples of companies that had been left for dead by the market. They are companies that I purchased as part of the October 2012 reset of the 52-Week Low strategy and companies that I think perfectly illustrate

---

*Howard Marks, *The Most Important Thing* (New York: Columbia University Press, 2011).

the way a disciplined, logical, data-centric approach to investing can and will help you overcome popular biases to discover opportunity. They are proof positive that a smart investor welcomes negative sentiment during the period of evaluation and inclusion process. If sentiment surrounding a company is positive, chances are good you will overpay for it.

All three of these companies were in the headlines around the time of the reset. In all three cases, the headlines weren't good. But all three of the companies passed the five filters of the 52-Week Low strategy and yielded tremendous results for my clients.

Company 1: Best Buy

There was a time, before Amazon and iTunes, when Best Buy seemed like the golden goose—only instead of laying golden eggs, it was selling gold records. The company was synonymous with personal electronics and personal media, and it seemed like the sky was the limit.

Then came the iPod, the iPhone, and cultural shift that seemed to sound the death knell for this big box electronic behemoth. In the fall of 2012, when the world was reading the biography of Steve Jobs on its Kindles, sentiment toward Best Buy took a decidedly sour turn. And had the 52-Week Low strategy not been in place, there's a good chance I would never have bought the company.

But let's look at how the company stacked up against the five filters of the 52-Week Low.

Filter 1: Durable Competitive Advantage

Does the company have an advantage over digital retail? Absolutely. People who buy 60-inch plasma TVs and washers and driers online and pay to have them shipped are fairly uncommon. And among the brick-and-mortar retailers, Best Buy had the advantage of scale and, believe it or not, had achieved a consistent ROIC in excess of its COC over a 10-year period.

Filter 2: Free Cash Flow Yield

FCF yield: 12.87 percent

The company definitely provided a margin of safety as its FCF Yield provided quite a multiple over the 2.65 percent return of a 10-year Treasury bond, known as the risk-free rate.

Filter 3: Return on Invested Capital

ROIC: 21.42 percent

The current ROIC being achieved was above its COC.

Filter 4: Long-Term Debt to Free Cash Flow

The long-term debt coverage (long-term debt/FCF) for Best Buy was 0.67x, which meant it would take the company less than seven months to pay off all its debts in case of emergency.

Filter 5: 52-Week Low

Was Best Buy at or near its 52-Week Low in the fall of 2012? Absolutely. At the time it was added to the strategy, it was up only 3.4 percent over its 52-Week Low at $17.91.

So, how did it do? Did Best Buy make for a good investment decision? You be the judge (Figure 9.1).

In one year's time, the stock that had all but been abandoned by Wall Street had a 119.21 percent price return as of October 11, 2013, reaching $39.26. And what happened to popular sentiment? Well, you can guess, but let's just say that a year after the company fit the 52-Week Low model and investors everywhere seemed to be decrying it, things had turned around. The sentiment was severely low when it was added to the strategy and was quite high when it was removed from the strategy.

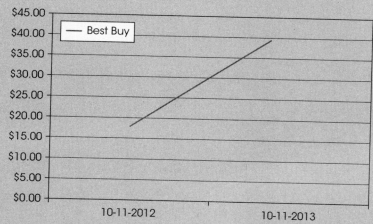

Figure 9.1   Best Buy

(continued)

(continued)

Company 2: Flir Sytems

Unlike Best Buy, which holds a certain spot in the popular awareness, thermal imaging companies are not often talked about at water coolers or by the talking heads looking for someone to skewer as an example of the way technology has changed our lives. But investor sentiment toward Flir Systems had certainly cooled in the fall of 2012, and it seemed like the market was walking away.

Filter 1: Durable Competitive Advantage

The company had consistently earned above its COC for a decade and had clear competitive advantages in the sector.

Filter 2: Free Cash Flow Yield

FCF yield: 8.25 percent
    Not quite as dramatic as Best Buy, but still well worth the risk as compared to Treasury bonds (risk-free rate of 2.65 percent). Flir Systems was providing three times the free cash flow of a Treasury bond.

Filter 3: Return on Invested Capital

ROIC: 15.82 percent
    The management team at Flir had consistently delivered ROIC in the teens, indicating quality decision making.

Filter 4: Long-Term Debt to Free Cash Flow

LTD coverage: −0.80x years
    The company had more than enough cash on hand to cover its long-term debts without dipping into free cash flow—an excellent sign of opportunity.

Filter 5: 52-Week Low

As of October 11, 2012, Flir Systems was 8 percent from its 52-Week Low at $19.79 per share.
    In just one year, Flir Systems delivered a 65.08 percent price return, reaching $32.67 on October 11, 2013 (Figure 9.2).

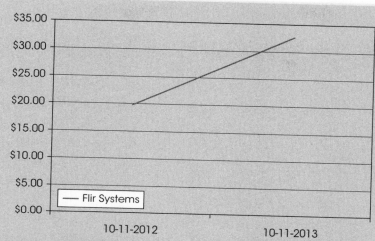

Figure 9.2   Flir Systems

Company 3: Johnson & Johnson

This was another company that passed the filters of the 52-Week Low strategy in the fall of 2012. Johnson & Johnson is one of the (if not the) largest and most profitable health care companies in the world, but investors had lost interest around the time of the strategy reset, creating an opportunity for disciplined investors seeking value over popularity.

Filter 1: Durable Competitive Advantage

This should go without saying. Johnson & Johnson has long been an industry leader, but I still confirmed its near-term and long-term fundamental metrics to ensure it truly was a company with durability.

Filter 2: Free Cash Flow Yield

FCF: 6.51 percent

Not as high as other companies, but with Johnson & Johnson, the risk is not as great, and so the potential reward doesn't need to be quite as high, though it had a multiplied upside over the Treasury bond (more than double the risk-free rate).

(continued)

(*continued*)

Filter 3: Return on Invested Capital

ROIC: 17.55

Consistency is king here. Johnson & Johnson has demonstrable history of ROIC being greater than its COC.

Filter 4: Long-Term Debt to Free Cash Flow

LTD coverage: −0.20x years

Not surprising, given the company's size and history, but still noteworthy that Johnson & Johnson could, at this time, effectively write a check for its debt and still have money in the bank without using any free cash flow.

Filter 5: 52-Week Low

The stock as of October 11, 2012 was trading 9.9 percent from its 52-Week Low at $67.99.

Just one year later, on October 11, 2013, the stock closed at $89.45 per share at the close of business, a 31.56 percent price return (Figure 9.3).

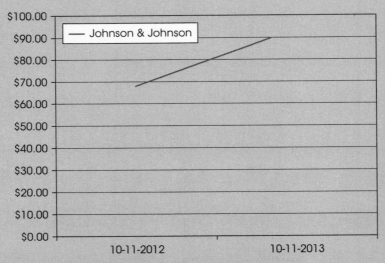

Figure 9.3   Johnson & Johnson

All three of these stocks were evaluated for taxable accounts, which are reset every 12 months as part of the 52-Week Low strategy, and all three had a few things in common:

- Sentiment was bad, but it didn't matter. These stocks were identified based on data, not headlines.
- All three, despite being in radically different sectors, were evaluated the same way. There were no free passes for popularity, price, or size. All three had to pass the five filters of the 52-Week Low.
- All three outperformed the market for the year they were in the strategy, and all three were sold when they no longer passed the filters when it was time to reset.

Had you bought just a single share of each of the three companies on October 11, 2012, you would have spent $105.69. A year later, those shares would be worth $161.38, a gain of nearly 53 percent (Figure 9.4).

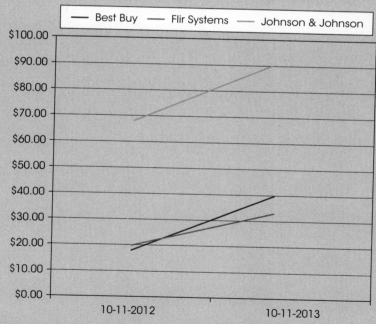

Figure 9.4   Best Buy, Flir Systems, and Johnson & Johnson

(continued)

(continued)

Of course, these were just three of the 25 stocks that made up the strategy that year, and not all of them performed as well. In fact, 20 of the 25 grew, and five lost value. This is important to note, not only because it reveals the fact that the "batting average" of the companies that make up the 52-Week Low every 6 to 12 months is between 70 percent and 80 percent in terms of those that grow compared to those that lose, but because it shows how wrong popular sentiment can be.

When it comes to a proper investment strategy, it's much better to make decisions based on what you can know, not just what you hear.

CHAPTER 10

The Sunk-Cost Bias and Pride and Regret

*J*acobian Inverse: *If I have decided to build a plane and I've sunk $100 million into a $2 billion project, come hell or high water I'm going to build this plane, no matter what. Even if my closest competitor beats me to the market, charges less, and builds a better plane, I will still see it through; after all, I've already spent $100 million on it. I cannot be willing to look at my investment position with a fresh pair of eyes; rather, I will maintain the same course of action no matter what.*

If I want to make good investment decisions, I need to be objective and dispassionate. In order to ensure I don't do that, I should make decisions based on emotional attachment, pride, and stubbornness. I am simply unwilling to let go and move on.

Let's walk through a scenario. Let's say I'm an airplane manufacturer and I've decided to build the plane that will make the *Dreamliner* look like a rowboat. I've crunched the numbers and come to the conclusion that the potential revenue from such a plane is roughly $2 billion. Airlines and oligarchs all over the world are clamoring for my new plane. A rough sketch was leaked on the Internet, and, overnight, the phones started ringing. The only problem? I have to build it.

So I gather my engineers, aeronautics experts, and manufacturing team, and we begin planning, designing, and building the plane. It has everything—a floor reserved for parents flying with children, a pet hotel for travelers who can't leave Fifi behind. We're even exploring the logistics of an onboard health club (with a pool!). We're halfway through the build when our chief financial officer knocks on my door with some tough news. We're only halfway through the build, and we've already spent more than $1.5 billion. Gulp. Finishing the project will require at least another billion in capital.

If you were me, what would you do?

Do you continue on and create the vehicle that will change transcontinental travel forever? Or do you look at the numbers and walk away?

Logic, and my own projections, would tell me that finishing the plane, no matter how wonderful, is a losing proposition—a $500 million losing proposition. To finish the airplane would mean to cave to ego and pride of creation, forging ahead to what is undoubtedly a losing proposition. My hope is that, if you're reading this, you saw the way forward clearly. You knew that the only smart thing to do would be to walk away.

With the airplane example, the right answer is obvious for a couple of reasons: (1) because the scale is huge, and just as a caricature uses inflated scale to highlight specific features of a person's face, massive amounts of money make these kinds of choices easy; and (2) it wasn't your money, it was mine. We are hardwired to remove ourselves and see the logical flaws of others. But when it comes to turning that magnifying glass back on our own lives, it gets clouded. Emotions, fear, social and peer pressure—all of these things get in the way of our seeing our own clear logical flaws.

Investing and retirement planning are no different. We invest in funds and stocks with a certain expectation for return. And without having a clear and disciplined strategy in place, we will continue to pour money into those instruments with the hope that we will meet those initial expectations.

In behavioral and investment psychology circles, it's called the *sunk-cost bias*. It goes a little something like this:

I invest A amount with the anticipation of a C return.

I continue to invest, even though the return is only B.

Wanting for that C return and afraid that my initial A investment will be for naught, I continue to invest, even though the actual return continues to be elusive.

The point is this: In order to avoid chasing good money with bad in pursuit of something, it's important to have a strategy and discipline in place that forces you to review progress and make sound, logical decisions. You also need someone in place to help make those decisions for you.

This is a core tenet of the 52-Week Low formula, a rigid 6- and 12-month review process where we sit down and start over. Every 6 months, we identify the stocks that meet our criteria and start over. About 85 times out of 100, this will mean divesting of the stocks we bought 6 months before—remember, the final filter is to find companies trading near their 52-Week Low—taking our gains and building on them. We're not building a super-plane here, we're planning and providing for your future, and the last thing you need is a clouded lens.

Two important forces in behavioral finance are the same forces that influence many of the decisions we make in life: pride and regret. Pride can fool us into making poor decisions even when the right option is so clearly in front of us. Regret often blinds us to success because our expectations were somehow formed by a previous experience.

In June 2008, UBS Wealth Management Research published a white paper[1] on influential forces of behavioral

---

[1]Joachim Klement, Veronica Weisser, and Thomas Wacker, "Behavioral Finance: Where Your Mind Can Play Tricks on You When You Invest—and What You Can Do about It," UBS Wealth Management Research, 2008.

finance. Pride and regret were addressed directly through the following example (paraphrased for clarity):

> Bob invests money in a stock that's trading at $50 per share. A year later, the stock is trading at $100 per share. What does Bob do? Well, without a process and discipline in place to force him to sell, Bob is left to make a decision on his own. He believes the stock will continue to rise. His pride is blinding him to the reality that a stock that has doubled in price in 12 months is going to be popular, its value may be—most likely is—overinflated, and expecting additional growth is risky. Still, he decides to hold on to the stock.
>
> Six months later, the stock price has fallen to $75 per share and Bob finally makes the decision to sell. An outsider would look at what Bob has done—gained 50 percent of his initial investment in 18 months—and be impressed. But Bob can't be satisfied by the move. Why? Because he could have sold it for $100 but didn't. This regret blinds Bob to the impressive gain because it was only half of what it could have been.

What is interesting about pride, regret, and the sunk cost basis is that you can have a gain on a stock but still be anchored on its highest price while you have owned it. There are thousands of homeowners who paid $250,000 in the late 1990s for 3 to 4 bedroom condominiums on the beaches of Destin, Florida and watched their values soar anywhere from $800,000 to $1,000,000 by mid-2007. Did many of them sell their condos then, or even now? Even though these condos might be currently valued at $500,000, these homeowners think they are down $500,000 because they are anchoring on the highest value of the condo and not on the fact that they have doubled their return on the condo. The reference point should be the purchase price, which was $250,000, and not the all-time high of the investment. When it comes to investing, you must be at peace with the fact that rarely will you sell a stock at its all-time high and rarely will you buy a stock at its all-time low.

"Could have been" is as dangerous as "might become" in investing. They are two sides of the same emotional coin. "Could have been" is regret. "Might become" is pride. Both are emotions—emotions that cloud our decision making ability. What's the likelihood that Bob will expect similar gains from future investments? Well, if it's based on his pride in the 100 percent year 1 increase, then it's pretty likely. What's the likelihood that he'll be a bit more trigger-happy to sell when a future investment is rising? Pretty high, because that regret from missing the opportunity to double his money will linger in the back of his mind and in his heart.

The head and the heart are incredible things, but they can keep people up at night or give them a false sense of comfort and stability. To be sure, a lot of money has been made in the markets over the years based on hunches, intuition, and pride. But just as much has probably been lost. Disciplined, systems-based investing is about eliminating pride and regret and making good decisions for pragmatic reasons.

It takes focus and discipline to not ask yourself what could have been or what something might become. In the end, the only questions that will matter as it relates to your wealth are: What was it? And, what is it? Anything else is pride and regret.

11

Filter 5: The 52-Week Low Formula and My Journey Trying to Disprove It

*J*acobian Inverse: *If I want to ensure that I minimize my likely return on an investment, I will focus on buying stocks that are trading at their 52-Week Highs. I will identify the stocks in highest demand and join the surplus of buyers clamoring for shares. I will put a lot of money into a stock in the hopes of incremental—or possibly negative—gains. I will buy high and hope for slightly higher, even at the risk of selling low.*

The fifth and final filter of the 52-Week Low strategy is designed to identify companies trading below their historic and recent high prices, companies with more sellers than buyers. Buying low and selling high is Economics 101 thinking, but it constantly amazes me how often this cardinal and basic rule is overlooked or that breaking it is so easily justified by investors and firms.

The fact that this simple rule is so often broken reveals how cognitive biases and emotional influences work against our better judgment when it comes to investing. We see a company's stock rising and we get a sense that we should be investing in it. We watch it rise, we watch people making money, and we want a piece of the action. We see Apple setting new company records and our knee-jerk reaction is to invest. We justify our actions. Everyone else seems to be making money there, so we can make money there. We see week after week of gains and believe this is the right time. We buy. It will continue to rise, right? It has to. It must continue to rise. There must be money to be made there. We say all these things and more to ourselves. We believe it will continue to grow. We have faith in it.

And that's the problem.

Investing your money should not be a matter of faith or belief. It should not be based on a feeling or a headline. If you have learned anything by this point in this book, I hope it is this: When it comes to investments, the only way to mitigate risk and protect your future gains is to have a system that is based on what is known—not what is felt, assumed, or hoped for, but known. Strategies protect us from our lesser natures, those parts of us that want to follow a crowd, that believe in a trend, that keep us amid a sea of buyers in a seller's market. Strategies and rigorous adherence to them eliminate the need to justify. If you have a process for making decisions and stick to that process, then there is no need to justify anything. The process is the justification. You can stop fretting about whether you should have made another decision and spend that energy doing something more productive.

If you want to invest in Apple or another "hot" stock because you are curious about it, either as an academic exercise or because you are the kind of person who likes to sit down at a blackjack table and see how the cards fall, fine. But there's a rule smart people follow when they head to the casinos: never bet money you aren't prepared to lose. You don't bring your retirement savings to a weekend in Vegas, so why bet your nest egg on the most crowded corners of the market?

The sequence of the filters in the 52-Week Low strategy is as important as the filters themselves. There's a good reason they are in the order that they are. The order helps to take the thousands of companies listed on the New York Stock Exchange and winnow them down from big to small. The filters are how we take 3,000 companies and identify the 25 that present the best value and greatest chances of growth over a 6- or 12-month period.

A little review before we move on:

Filter 1: Durable Competitive Advantage

- Is the company in an industry with good economics? Are revenues dictated by customers or vendors? Is it a saturated industry in which the company is easily replaceable?
- Has the company demonstrated a consistency of generating returns on capital over its cost of capital over a full business cycle?
- Does the company appear to have an economic moat that will allow it to fend off competition?

Filter 2: Free Cash Flow Yield

- Does the company create free cash flow sufficient to allow for cash distribution and/or reinvestment while maintaining its competitiveness in the marketplace?
- Does it have not only positive free cash flow, but enough of a margin of safety or opportunity for excess cash flow over the risk-free rate to justify the investment risk?

Filter 3: Return on Invested Capital

- Does the company invest money in such a way that it generates returns on capital above its cost of capital in the current environment?

Filter 4: Long-Term Debt to Free Cash Flow Ratio

- If something catastrophic happens, can the company service its debts and maintain its production capacity?
- Can the company pay off its long-term debt with its free cash flow within three years?

These first four filters serve to identify companies that compete in industries with good economics, are generators of free cash flow in excess of the risk-free rate, achieve returns on capital exceeding their cost of capital, have very good balance sheets to justify investment, and have good management and staying power in the short term. So, what does the last filter do? It helps to identify the best opportunities now, right now, for the next six months—the 25 companies that represent the best value.

Too often, value is viewed by investors as a dirty word. They associate a value strategy as somehow being tied solely to price. But value has little to do with price and everything to do with potential. Value can be defined as the place where expectations and opportunity meet (Figure 11.1).

The expectation you have when you invest your money is that the money you put into your investments will grow, that you will benefit from the investments in the form of gains. Identifying the opportunities of investing is what the 52-Week Low strategy is all about—following a series of consistent rules

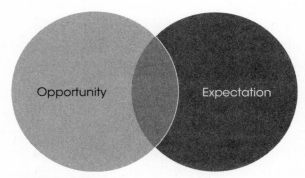

Figure 11.1 The Definition of Value

(filters) that help to discover opportunities without the cloud of emotion or justification.

And the opportunities cemented by the fifth filter are in those companies where the crowds of buyers have dispersed and you are left with just sellers. When there are more buyers than sellers, prices rise. Where there are equal numbers of sellers and buyers, prices stagnate. However, where there are fewer buyers than sellers, prices fall. It is that simple, but that simplicity is vital to successful investing.

A Matter of Timing

The 52-Week Low strategy is about building value over time. In almost every instance, when reviewing the data of each company as part of the filtering process, we are looking at the consistency of return on invested capital (ROIC) in excess of cost of capital (COC) over a full business cycle, as well as a snapshot of ROIC over COC. We are looking at the current free cash flow (FCF) yield at a multiple over the risk-free rate. And the final filter is no different, except we are looking at a set of data from a single year to identify those companies that are trading at or very close to their one-year lows. This helps to ensure that we are not only buying companies with signs of a durable competitive advantage and a margin of safety but also trying to buy these quality businesses as low as possible from a valuation and enthusiasm standpoint, creating a *behavioral advantage*, as Russell Fuller, CFA, would call it,[1] that should increase the probability for outperformance.

My Journey of Skepticism

Even though our clients and our team had been having success buying good businesses that were trading around their 52-Week Lows, I had to be willing to let the data speak for

---

[1] Russell J. Fuller, CFA, "Behavioral Finance and the Sources of Alpha," February 6, 2000, www.fullerthaler.com/downloads/bfsoa.pdf.

itself. So, I asked Morningstar to run several independent back tests to disprove or further prove the 52-Week Low formula. One of the first back tests was to isolate price, comparing the 25 companies trading closest to their 52-Week Highs versus buying the companies trading closest to their 52-Week Lows with a six-month rebalance.

Would I have been better off buying businesses where the public sentiment was quite positive with companies trading around their 52-Week Highs or better off buying businesses where the public sentiment was quite low with companies trading around their 52-Week Lows?

The 52-Week Low prevailed, and the details follow.

The case study from independent back-testing of the 52-Week Low strategy[2] compares what happens if you invested $1 million into two sets of 25 companies in April 2004. None of the 52-Week Low strategy filters were applied. The only thing studied was the impact of price. The first group was trading at or near 52-Week Highs in April of that year, while the second set was trading at or near 52-Week Lows. The total gains in both instances reflect a 1 percent management fee, and dividend distributions in both cases will be noted.

The testing reveals just how important timing and enthusiasm are to identifying real opportunity. It's one thing to identify a quality company. It's quite another to identify that same company when it has the most to gain (see Figure 11.2 and Table 11.1).

As you can see in Figure 11.2, the companies bought at their 52-Week Highs initially outperformed those bought at the 52-Week Lows, but during the market crash of 2008, the 52-Week High portfolio value fell further and took longer to recover. In the long run, those companies trading at their lows presented a better value and gained money, thanks to a shorter recovery period from the economic crisis to produce gains over the initial investment. It's important to note that none of the 50

---

[2] Conducted by Morningstar, CPMS Back Test, January 14, 2014.

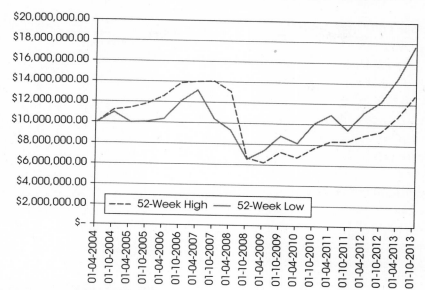

Figure 11.2   52-Week High versus 52-Week Low, Without Filters
Conducted by Morningstar CPMS Back Test, January 14, 2014.

Table 11.1   52-Week High versus 52-Week Low, Without Filters

Price Only—52-Week High without Filters

52 Week Hi—No Strategy

Performance Statistics	Portfolio	Benchmark	Net
Annualized Returns			
Since Inception	2.75%	7.66%	−4.91%
1-Yr Return	37.10%	32.39%	4.71%
3-Yr Return	18.70%	16.18%	2.52%
5-Yr Return	13.89%	17.94%	−4.05%
10-Yr Return	n/a	n/a	

Best/Worst	Portfolio	Benchmark
Best 3m Return	12.68%	25.83%
Worst 3m Return	−37.45%	−29.65%
Best 6m Return	19.28%	40.52%
Worst 6m Return	−49.01%	−41.82%

(continued)

Table 11.1   *(continued)*

Best/Worst	Portfolio	Benchmark
Best 12m Return	37.10%	53.62%
Worst 12m Return	−55.57%	−43.32%
Max Drawdown (% of ptf value)	−62.56%	−50.95%
Period Start	Oct-07	Oct-07
Period End	Feb-09	Feb-09

Portfolio Stats (monthly)		
Alpha	−0.26	
Beta	0.82	
Pearson correlation coefficient (r)	0.82	
Coefficient of determination ($R2$)	0.67	
Turnover	186.49%	
Std Error	2.46	
Tstat	2.09	
Sharpe's measure	0.08	0.41
Treynor's measure	1.44	
Sortino ratio	0.23	0.73
Information ratio	−0.55	

Price Only—52-Week Low without Filters

52 Week Low—No Strategy

Performance Statistics	Portfolio	Benchmark	Net
Annualized Returns			
Since Inception	6.49%	7.66%	−1.17%
1-Yr Return	44.12%	32.39%	11.73%
3-Yr Return	20.75%	16.18%	4.57%
5-Yr Return	21.96%	17.94%	4.02%
10-Yr Return	n/a	n/a	

Best/Worst	Portfolio	Benchmark
Best 3m Return	28.63%	25.83%
Worst 3m Return	−36.36%	−29.65%
Best 6m Return	41.13%	40.52%
Worst 6m Return	−43.80%	−41.82%

Table 11.1   *(continued)*

Best/Worst	Portfolio	Benchmark
Best 12m Return	56.20%	53.62%
Worst 12m Return	−43.41%	−43.32%
Max Drawdown (% of ptf value)	−57.35%	−50.95%
Period Start	May-07	Oct-07
Period End	Feb-09	Feb-09

Portfolio Stats (monthly)		
Alpha	−0.08	
Beta	1.05	
Pearson correlation coefficient (r)	0.87	
Coefficient of determination ($R2$)	0.76	
Turnover	175.56%	
Std Error	2.53	
Tstat	0.68	
Sharpe's measure	0.27	0.41
Treynor's measure	4.67	
Sortino ratio	0.51	0.73
Information ratio	−0.13	

Conducted by Morningstar CPMS Back Test, January 14, 2014.

companies (25 stocks per strategy)—both high and low—had passed the initial four filters.[3] It was only on price alone—those companies trading closest to their 52 Week Highs versus those companies trading closest to their 52-Week Lows.

I was still skeptical, despite the data in Table 11.1, because I was questioning the application of the four quantitative value filters to those trading closest to their 52 Week Highs—would that strategy outperform versus applying the four quantitative filters to those trading closest to their 52-Week Lows?

The 52-Week Low prevailed again, and the results are shown in Table 11.2 and Figure 11.3.

---

[3]Refer to the 52-Week Low and recovery case study in Chapter 5.

Table 11.2   52-Week High versus 52-Week Low, With Filters

52-Week High with Filters

Performance Statistics	Portfolio	Benchmark	Net
Annualized Returns			
Since Inception	11.73%	7.66%	4.07%
1-Yr Return	36.32%	32.39%	3.94%
3-Yr Return	18.45%	16.18%	2.27%
5-Yr Return	18.52%	17.94%	0.58%
10-Yr Return	n/a	n/a	

Best/Worst	Portfolio	Benchmark
Best 3m Return	26.09%	25.83%
Worst 3m Return	−29.59%	−29.65%
Best 6m Return	34.50%	40.52%
Worst 6m Return	−39.19%	−41.82%
Best 12m Return	47.55%	53.62%
Worst 12m Return	−36.45%	−43.32%

Max Drawdown (% of ptf value)	−41.66%	−50.95%
Period Start	May-07	Oct-07
Period End	Feb-09	Feb-09

Portfolio Stats (monthly)		
Alpha	0.38	
Beta	0.90	
Pearson correlation coefficient (r)	0.90	
Coefficient of determination ($R2$)	0.81	
Turnover	95.62%	
Std Error	1.85	
Tstat	3.18	
Sharpe's measure	0.69	0.41
Treynor's measure	11.28	
Sortino ratio	1.22	0.73
Information ratio	0.62	

Table 11.2   *(continued)*

52-Week Low with Filters

Performance Statistics	Portfolio	Benchmark	Net
Annualized Returns			
Since Inception	14.49%	7.66%	6.83%
1-Yr Return	34.97%	32.39%	2.58%
3-Yr Return	20.23%	16.18%	4.05%
5-Yr Return	23.43%	17.94%	5.49%
10-Yr Return	n/a	n/a	

Best/Worst	Portfolio	Benchmark
Best 3m Return	26.49%	25.83%
Worst 3m Return	−27.79%	−29.65%
Best 6m Return	40.06%	40.52%
Worst 6m Return	−31.05%	−41.82%
Best 12m Return	59.19%	53.62%
Worst 12m Return	−28.26%	−43.32%

Max Drawdown (% of ptf value)	−33.24%	−50.95%
Period Start	May-07	Oct-07
Period End	Feb-09	Feb-09

Portfolio Stats (monthly)

Alpha	0.61	
Beta	0.86	
Pearson correlation coefficient (r)	0.89	
Coefficient of determination (R2)	0.80	
Turnover	115.83%	
Std Error	1.88	
Tstat	4.86	
Sharpe's measure	0.90	0.41
Treynor's measure	14.96	
Sortino ratio	1.64	0.73
Information ratio	1.01	

---

*Conducted by Morningstar CPMS Back Test, January 14, 2014.

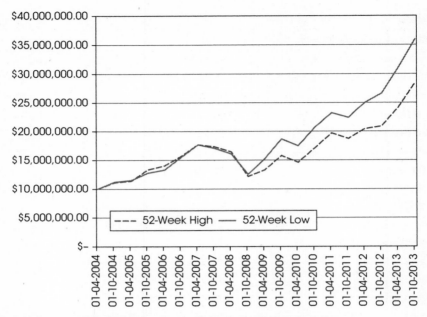

Figure 11.3   52-Week High versus 52-Week Low, with Filters
Conducted by Morningstar CPMS Back Test, January 14, 2014.

The question then becomes: why? Why did the companies trading at their highs fall so much more quickly and
take longer to recover than those trading at their 52-Week
Lows? Why did both analyses show a persistence of outperformance in both downside risk and portfolio growth when
applying the 52-Week Low price filter? It's a question of real
value—intrinsic value over relative value. Companies trading
at their highs are often trading beyond their actual values.
Their values are not reflective of their balance sheets but of
the demand being generated by buyers.

We know buyers do not always act rationally. They are
human, subject to biases like herding and the fear of missing out. It makes them chase crowded stocks. It makes them
take risks when risks are inappropriate. Collective behavior like this creates bubbles, and bubbles—all bubbles—are
bound to burst at some point. Those with a process in place

to overcome those biases tend to miss out on bubbles or, at the very least, recover more quickly after they burst.

The 52-Week Low formula is a pre-commitment strategy. Why is that important to self-control? James Montier talks about the power of pre-commitment as a means of acknowledging future bias. In other words, having a plan in place will keep you honest when temptation arises. By understanding your approach and maintaining devotion to process, you are less likely to get sucked in to fads, to succumb to herding, and to chase already overpriced businesses when sentiment is high.

Value-investing strategies like the 52-Week Low aren't just about finding good deals—they are about making logical choices. And those choices are largely made ahead of time. Is it intuitive to buy stocks that everyone else seems to be selling? No. But is it logical? Yes. While herding and the fear of missing out whip buyers into a frenzy and artificially inflate the price of a given stock or portfolio, the opposite is also true. Herding and the fear of getting stuck help sellers justify dumping a stock at a loss. It's the opposite of the sunk-cost bias. It's the rising loss bias that says, "Everyone else is selling; I better sell, too."

This leaves companies with an undervalued stock price with a much higher probability of recovery. It's rare for a stock to hit zero. And just as overinflated prices will eventually fall, underinflated ones should rise to meet the intrinsic value of the company. Recognizing this and buying when everyone else is selling is what separates a value investor from another true believer hoping a hot stock will continue to rise.

It's hard, cognitively and emotionally, to do this. It feels risky, I know. I've been there, but time and time again the process, the system, and the strategy have proven my gut feelings wrong. And I've come to realize that the key to outpacing the market with a value strategy is to learn to embrace and love the feeling of standing separate from the pack.

CHAPTER 12

The Importance of Embracing a Trailing 12-Month Return of −25 Percent

*J*acobian Inverse: *I want to seek out a portfolio of 25 businesses whose trailing 12-month returns are beyond great. Even though I did not participate in any of the prior performance, I want to put my principal into such a strategy. I want to err on the side of investing that gives me a higher probability that I am buying high. Why would anyone want to buy a business that is trading for less right now than it did in its recent past?*

I know the preceding paragraph sounds absurd, but this is the reality of the investing public and even most professionals. When you realize how ridiculous the mindset sounds, you realize that you want to welcome the fact that the companies you have identified to be in the strategy are trading much lower or substantially lower now than they did over the past 12 months.

Howard Marks said this:

The thing I find most interesting about investing is how paradoxical it is: how often the things that seem most

151

obvious—on which everyone agrees—turn out not to be true. . . . The ultimately most profitable investment actions are by definition contrarian: you're buying when everyone else is selling (and the price is thus low) or you're selling when everyoneelse is buying (and the price is high).[1]

This brings us to the reality of when you are resetting or establishing your own 52-Week Low strategy or, with the help of your adviser, realize—in fact, welcome—the fact that the trailing 12-month return of most of the companies in the new lineup have underwhelming returns.

In the fall of 2012, I was busy resetting the companies that make up the 52-Week Low strategy—evaluating those that passed the first four filters in the strategy and making final decisions about the 25 that would make the final cut—when I saw a number that sent shivers up my spine. As a younger man, those shivers would have been fear or doubt, but knowing what I know now, I recognized the unmistakable signs of real excitement.

The number was the trailing 12-month return of the collective portfolio benchmarked against the Standard & Poor's (S&P) 500. That number was −25.41 percent. The companies I was about to buy had underperformed the index by a little over 25 percent in the past 12 months. Collectively, they had lost 2.84 percent of their total value in a time when the market had shown a 22.57 percent gain. I could not have been more excited.

In fact, if you were to look just at the companies with negative 12-month trailing returns (see Figure 11.3 in Chapter 11), collectively they lost 12.79 percent while the market had shown a trailing 12-month total return of 22.57 percent. Six months later, those same companies returned 17.89 percent while the S&P had returned 12.48 percent.

[1] Howard Marks, *The Most Important Thing* (New York: Columbia University Press, 2011).

Why? Because over the past two decades, I had learned to embrace the negative and see it for what it really was: upside and opportunity. It's completely counterintuitive. I mean, if you were drafting a baseball team and, when your lineup was established, you were told that your players had hit 25 percent fewer home runs than your opponents, you might get nervous. That's conventional wisdom. That seems like a no-brainer. Fewer home runs must equate to fewer wins, right?

Wrong.

Just as Michael Lewis detailed in *Moneyball,* I knew something about those companies that the Oakland A's knew about their roster of no-name players: They may not hit as many home runs, but they give up fewer runs, make fewer errors, and score more runs with singles and walks than anyone else in baseball, and, most important, they will cost me less money in contracts and incentives.[2]

The companies on my screen had passed the first four filters. They were good companies that had been left behind by the fads, just like the players on those A's teams were good players who were no longer considered superstars. The players and the companies weren't sexy, but they got the job done. And when it comes to baseball and investing, sexy isn't nearly as important as getting a job done well.

Take a look at what I saw on my screen that day in October 2012 (Figure 12.1).

Not exactly a confidence booster, right? If I were to take a seventh grader out of economics class and show him this and ask him if I should invest, chances are pretty good he'd roll his eyes and walk away. And why not? This is pretty ugly. If you were to glance at this list of companies, it wouldn't be hard to pass. That's understandable. It's human nature. Just like those

---

[2]Jim Fink, "Moneyball and Value Investing: Variant Perception is Key to Success," *Investing Daily,* November 15, 2013, www.investingdaily.com/18790/moneyball-and -value-investing-variantperception-is-key-to-success/.

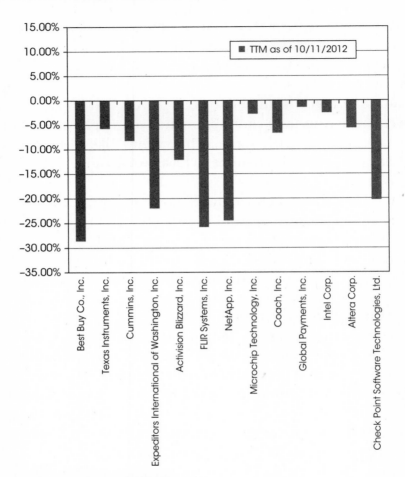

Figure 12.1   Trailing 12 Months

baseball players whose individual stats wouldn't exactly qualify them for a Wheaties box, these stocks look tired and over the hill. Even the companies themselves may create a visceral reaction or repulsion. Best Buy? Bed Bath & Beyond? Aren't these doomed for the Blockbuster Video list of companies made extinct by the Internet?

They are, in short, not pretty.

If you used the trailing 12-month performance—or name association—as the indicator of opportunity, you'd run. But I, and hopefully you, did not see this at a glance but as the final review of a rigorous process. Those trailing returns represented the final filter in the process of review, and, to my mind, they represented a tremendous opportunity. Figure 12.2 shows what happened when I reviewed performance the following April while resetting the strategy.

At the time these companies were added into the strategy, enthusiasm was low—almost nonexistent. These companies

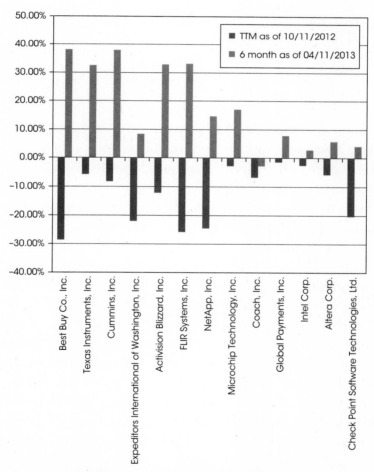

Figure 12.2   Trailing 12 Months versus Following 6 Months in the Strategy

Table 12.1   The Turnaround Results from Figure 12.1

	TTM	6 months later
Best Buy	−28.59%	38.09%
Texas Instruments	−5.74%	32.53%
Cummins	−8.21%	37.92%
Expeditors International	−21.97%	8.43%
Check Point Software Technologies Ltd.	−20.30%	4.09%
Activation Blizzard	−12.13%	32.93%
Flir Systems	−25.76%	33.17%
NetApp	−24.48%	14.66%
Microchip Technology	−2.77%	17.01%
Coach	−6.69%	−2.77%
Global Payments	−1.41%	7.91%
Intel	−2.56%	2.80%
Altera Corp.	−5.68%	5.81%

Data from S&P Capital IQ.

had been hammered, and everyone who was going to sell had already done so. Now, six months later, do you think enthusiasm was high? Of course it was, which is why we sell them and start all over again.

Take a closer look at the amazing turnaround that happened for the companies with negative returns going into the strategy (Table 12.1).

At the time these companies were added to the strategy, popular opinion on them was low—with good reason. However, over the following six-month period, the portfolio as a whole (with all 25 companies) returned 19.11 percent, exceeding the S&P's 12.48 percent return by nearly 7 percent. The question you have to ask yourself as an investor is this: What is the value of popular opinion?

"The error is clear," Marks once said. "The herd applies optimism at the top and pessimism at the bottom. Thus, to benefit, we must be skeptical of the optimism that thrives at the top, and skeptical of the pessimism that prevails at the bottom."[3]

---

[3] Marks, *The Most Important Thing*.

Popular opinion helps guide our decisions all the time. Is that new movie good? Ask your friend who has seen it before you decide whether to go. Popular opinion, in most cases, is a great tool for helping us figure out what comes next. Popular opinion dictates elections and drives fashion and food, branding and marketing.

Fifty million Elvis fans can't be wrong, and, apparently, they weren't.

As an investor, the value of popular opinion is often in its inverse. You want companies to be unpopular to understand the opportunities they represent. You want to avoid the most popular companies people are clamoring to get "in on" because demand drives prices upward. It's simple economics.

The reason the companies highlighted earlier had the capacity for amazing growth was twofold:

1. They were structurally sound companies that had passed the first four filters of the 52-Week Low strategy.
2. They were unpopular companies, companies where demand had slackened to a crawl, driving prices below their intrinsic value.

If you ever watch baseball, you'll hear a phrase every once in a while related to a team's best power hitter who's in a slump. "He's due," the announcer says, and the sentiment is repeated on the breaths of hopeful fans everywhere. The implication is that this hitter has a proven track record of performance that, although he is in a dry spell, is reason enough to believe that on any given pitch, he'll send one over the outfield wall and win the game.

It's easy to mistake what I'm covering here with that sort of blind hope. It is not the same thing. The 52-Week Low strategy hits its fair share of home runs, but we are trying for singles, walks, and balks. We are managing consistency in the often unpredictable construct of the market. We are using

Sabermetrics in the age of the home-run hitter. We don't look at a stock that's in a dry spell and hope that it will return to its former glory. Instead, we look at an overlooked, undervalued stock with a track record of consistent performance and a clean bill of health. If they are in a slump, the opportunity is even better. And we don't send them out there to hit a game-winning home run. We send them out there to bunt in the top of the second.

Baseball analogies aside, the point here is to identify good companies first and then look for those good companies that have underperformed and are undervalued as opportunities. The 52-Week Low strategy is designed to do just that.

At this point in the book, I hope you are questioning these results. Trusting, but wanting to verify. But when it comes to this idea of embracing structurally sound losers, I want you, the reader, to understand its value.

I reset the 52-Week Low strategy twice a year (once a year for large, taxable accounts). The ones I selected in October 2012 were obviously winners dressed in loser clothing. But what happened six months later in April when it was time to reset? Were the trailing returns as big a nightmare? Did those companies perform as well?

Let's take a look.

Table 12.2 lists the companies that qualified for the 52-Week Low strategy reset in April 2013 and their trailing 12 months of returns. Figure 12.3 shows just how badly these companies had been performing.

Were the results from October 2012 to April 2013 outliers? Could the process and the strategy return similar results? The short answer is yes (see Table 12.3).

Following the reset, the newly selected companies' trailing 12-month returns had underperformed the S&P 500 by 22.64 percent. Now, six months later, they yet again outperformed

Table 12.2   Trailing 12 Months of Returns from April 2013

Company	Trailing 12 months
Apple, Inc.	−29.65%
Avago Technolgies Ltd.	−2.00%
Baidu, Inc.	−37.63%
Check Point Software*	−22.88%
Garmin Ltd.	−19.00%
Infosys Ltd.	−3.98%
Skyworks Solutions, Inc.	−15.18%
Altera Corp.	−7.51%
Citrix Systems, Inc.	−6.73%
EMC Corp.	−17.76%
F5 Networks, Inc.	−42.79%
NVIDIA Corp.	−8.25%
Teva Pharmaceutical	−9.03%

*This was a company that was carried over from the fall 2012 reset, though it still went through the same filters in the spring of 2013.
Data from S&P Capital IQ

the market. In this six-month period, the companies selected for the strategy produced a return of 14.5 percent, while the S&P 500 returned 7.76 percent.

In fact, looking again at just the companies with negative 12-month returns (Table 12.3, Figure 12.4), you'll see that they collectively lost 17.11 percent while the market had shown a trailing 12-month total return of 19.54 percent. Six months later, those same companies returned 17.62 percent while the S&P returned 7.76 percent. So, at the point the companies were added, their trailing 12-month return had underperformed the market by 36.65 percent, and six months later it outperformed the market by almost 10 percent.

Nothing is guaranteed in investing, but these results show a high persistence of previous underperformance turning into positive performance. I would encourage you to go to 52weeklow.com to read the back-test data from Morningstar and Empiritrage to see for yourself. The 52-Week Low formula is designed to find winners in stocks that have

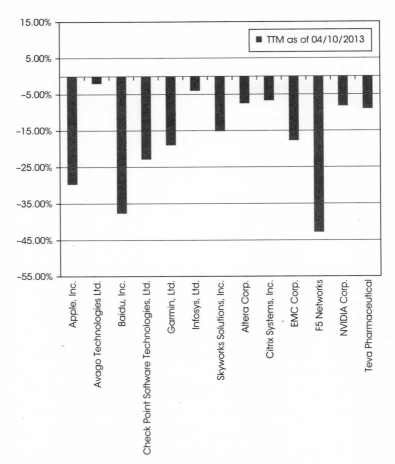

Figure 12.3 Trailing 12 Months as of April 10, 2013
Data from S&P Capital IQ.

underperformed and are underwhelming in the year leading up to their addition to the strategy.

Why is this important? Because it's important to distinguish between companies that have underperformed and those that are undervalued. Undervalued stocks usually have underperformed. It's one of the reasons they are undervalued. But not all underperforming stocks are undervalued. Some companies haven't performed well because they are unstable or unsound. *The 52-Week Low filters seek to weed*

Table 12.3   The Turnaround Results from Figure 11.7

	TTM	6 months later
Apple, Inc.	–29.65%	13.87%
Avago Technologies Ltd.	–2.00%	24.43%
Baidu, Inc.	–37.63%	70.05%
Check Point Software	–22.88%	19.95%
Garmin Ltd.	–19.00%	41.55%
Infosys Ltd.	–3.98%	–4.13%
Skyworks Solutions, Inc.	–15.18%	14.84%
Altera Corp.	–7.51%	9.73%
Citrix Systems, Inc.	–6.73%	–14.55%
EMC Corp.	–17.76%	9.16%
F5 Networks, Inc.	–42.79%	21.55%
NVIDIA Corp.	–8.25%	21.13%
Teva Pharmaceutical	–9.03%	5.41%

Data from S&P Capital IQ.

out those companies bound to continue losing from those that have lost and are primed for recovery. The key is to maintain the discipline of distinction. It's easy to rationalize that a company has passed four of the five filters—or three of the five—and is bound for a recovery. This is hope in the face of fear. You have to manage that rationalization, recognize it for what it is, and walk away. If a company fails even one of the filters and is trading at historic lows, there is probably a good reason beyond loss of popular sentiment.

The 52-Week Low strategy works very well, but it only works if you adhere to it. This means both rigidly demanding that all the companies pass all five of the filters *and* that you trust the five filters to turn the fear of negative trailing returns into realized opportunity. It's hard, particularly at first, to look at the numbers in red and see anything but loss. But you will learn, as I have, to embrace the trailing losses and even get excited by them.

As mentioned before, it's a little sadistic, I know, but going against the grain and seeking opportunity where others have

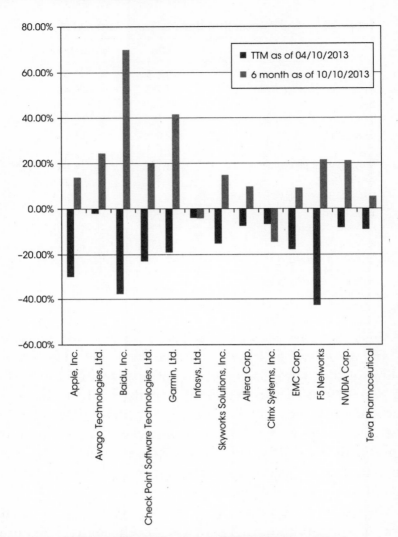

Figure 12.4   Trailing 12 months versus Following 6 months in the Strategy
Data from S&P Capital IQ.

abandoned their excitement is not without pain and discomfort. These pangs of discomfort are false. They are emotions disguising themselves as rationale. Maintain the process and stick to the strategy. Data, time, and results should prove the diligence worthwhile.

CHAPTER 13

The Problem with Selective Perception and Confirmation Basis

He who knows nothing is closer to the truth than he whose mind is filled with falsehoods and errors.

—Thomas Jefferson

The moment a person forms a theory, his imagination sees in every object only the traits which favor that theory.

—Thomas Jefferson

Jacobian Inverse: *When I watch the news, read research reports, listen to experts, or meet with analysts, I want to internalize and believe in only those insights that agree with my current beliefs. I would prefer to do this because it feels natural, congruent, and reaffirming. Why would I seek out data, facts, or insights that might cause me to possibly alter my current beliefs?*

We like to think of ourselves as objective, particularly as it relates to our investment decisions. We like to think we can remove ourselves from emotion and look at evidence in a cold, rational way. But, of course, we rarely can. We can rarely remove our own expectations—influenced by experience and biases based on our perceptions—and look at something completely for what it is without presupposing what we expect to see.

Let's say I want to know what the weather is going to be like this weekend. I see two people standing next to one another. One is an old friend, someone I have known for a very long time, someone I like and respect. The other is a person who, for one reason or another, I don't like. He is a rival. This person gets my hackles up or rubs me the wrong way. I approach them both and say, "Any idea what the weather is going to be like this weekend? I'm hoping to take my son, Jake, to a soccer game."

My friend says, "I heard it's going to be beautiful. Perfect weekend for a game."

My rival says, "The National Weather Service is calling for thunderstorms Saturday."

Which one will I believe? Chances are pretty good I'll believe my friend for a couple of reasons: (1) it's someone I know and trust, someone I value; and (2) what my friend said supported my hopes for the weekend weather—I am asking in the context of an event I am looking forward to attending, a soccer game with my son.

Now, let's go back and review what was actually said. My friend told me that he "heard it's going to be beautiful," while my rival cited the National Weather Service. Had I been truly objective in my inquiry, removing all source bias and hopes, the rival's answer is clearly more authoritative. It's outside factors that lead me to believe the friend over the rival, not the quality of information itself.

This is the problem of *selective perception*, when even our most objective of research becomes tainted by preference, bias, and aspiration without our knowing it. And selective perception can taint not only our weekend planning but our investing strategies and a whole host of other pursuits.

Don't believe me? Let's look at butter. For years, study after study seemed to come out saying that "butter is bad for you, don't eat it." Yet nearly every study that claims butter is bad for you has a twin from Bizarro World that says butter is fine, even healthy. Why would I choose to believe the latter? Well, because I love butter and want to eat it. My personal preference is to eat butter, and I will, consciously or unconsciously, seek information that validates my eating it.

Selective perception is part of human nature and is awfully hard to avoid completely, which is why former U.S. Vice President Charles Curtis put it best when he said, "Bias and prejudice are attitudes to be kept in hand, not attitudes to be avoided." You can never rid yourself of biases— they are part of what make you who you are. The key is in acknowledging their existence and checking your thoughts against them.

If a friend recommends an investment, do the same homework you would if you had discovered it yourself. Use opportunities like these to seek validation and avoid the pitfalls of selective perception by acknowledging its role in shaping your thoughts. At the end of the day, President Reagan had it right: "Trust, but verify."

One of the ways to help combat selective perception is to have someone you trust play devil's advocate when it comes to your investment decisions. Some of the best leaders and investors have team members whose role is to find all the reasons why the possible investment will not be fruitful. I would think it is safe to say that this type of relationship exists between Charlie Munger and Warren Buffett to ensure that they enhance their odds of thinking as clearly as possible.

Thankfully, I have this relationship with my partner and brother, Zach, whereby I ask him to challenge my thinking and how it could be incorrect. He will either find conflicting data or he will ask me more and more questions about my facts and thesis. This type of relationship can also exist between clients and their financial advisers. In seeking out the disadvantages of an investment in question, the truth should become more and more prevalent regarding the investment as worthwhile or inadequate.

When I reread Thomas Jefferson's quote, "The moment a person forms a theory, his imagination sees in every object only the traits which favor that theory," it reminds me how we all have a tendency to seek out information that reaffirms our deeply help beliefs and feelings about the world and its current environment. This is why when it comes to selecting the 25 companies for the 52-Week Low strategy, I pay zero attention to the buy or sell recommendations from analysts, because I know these recommendations might cloud my judgement. Not that I completely disregard analyst research; I don't. I find the most value in analyst research as it relates to the company's competitive position in the marketplace. This information helps me determine if the company has a durable competitive advantage (Filter 1 of the 52-Week Low formula) or not.

In fact, if you think about the 52-Week Low strategy, it is about identifying temporarily ill but healthy businesses that are trading closest to their 52-Week Lows. If you have a stock that is trading close to its 52-Week Low, is the stock often associated with good news and buy recommendations from the analyst community or is it associated with poor news, with several neutral, hold, or sell recommendations surrounding it? If I used the underwhelming stock price and the negative consensus viewpoint as my barometer (as most investors do), I would never buy most of the businesses that I should buy. Remember the cardinal rule of successful investing: Buy Low and Sell High. When you buy low, is the news surrounding the investment positive or negative?

Forbes published a paper titled, "How Warren Buffett Avoids Getting Trapped by Confirmation Bias,"[1] in which Buffett says:

> Charles Darwin used to say that whenever he ran into something that contradicted a conclusion he cherished, he was obliged to write the new finding down within 30 minutes. Otherwise his mind would work to reject the discordant information, much as the body rejects transplants. Man's natural inclination is to cling to his beliefs, particularly if they are reinforced by recent experience—a flaw in our makeup that bears on what happens during secular bull markets and extended periods of stagnation.

Buffett's point is that we often take comfort in numbers. We find ease in trends. It's this confirmation bias that leads us to make decisions based upon incomplete or inaccurate information. The saying goes that "50 million Elvis fans can't be wrong," but just because there are 50 million of them, it doesn't necessarily make them right, either. And just because it seems like the entire world has bought Apple, it doesn't necessarily mean buying Apple is the best decision.

Instead, when it seems like everyone you know is in agreement on something and you are inclined to follow, that is the moment when you need to be the most critical, to challenge your assumptions and beliefs for validity. After all, you might just realize that you don't like Elvis and that Apple doesn't fit well into your investment strategy.

The 52-Week Low is the antithesis of the confirmation bias. The whole process—the five filters—forces us to challenge

---

[1] Roger Dooley, "How Warren Buffett Avoids Getting Trapped by Confirmation Bias," *Forbes*, May 7, 2013, www.forbes.com/sites/rogerdooley/2013/05/07/buffett-confirmation-bias.

common wisdom. Even the process by which the formula was created—the Jacobian process of solving for the opposite of the desired result—forced me to challenge the accepted rules of investing, which is something I continue to do to this day. I would encourage you to do the same thing: to challenge my approach, challenge my thinking.

Mark Twain once said, "When you find yourself on the side of majority, it is time to pause and reflect." He was right. Not just because he believed the world was better with contrarians, but because he understood that popular opinion leads to complacency, and complacency is an impediment to progress and success.

CHAPTER 14

Putting It All Together

*J*acobian Inverse: *In order to limit my chances of investing success, I will do the following: have no strategy, let the present day be my guide, make emotional decisions, seek confirming data, eschew discipline, follow the crowd, invest in companies reaching new highs, and definitely take an "expert's" word for what to do about the future.*

There are around 2,800 companies listed on the New York Stock Exchange and roughly 5,000 companies on the Nasdaq. At any given time, some will be up and some will be down. Some of the stocks will be hotter than the core of the sun, and some will be devalued to the point that they are gasping for their last breaths. Wading through all the data and trying to predict the future of any given stock is a fool's errand. No one—I mean *no one*—can predict the future. But that doesn't mean you need to settle for the same old, same old when it comes to investing your money.

Most investors clamor to mutual funds or index funds because of fear of the perceived unknown, because there is safety in numbers—it feels comfortable, and the investment involves a high degree of cognitive ease. It's completely understandable, particularly when the alternative seems to be going rogue, flying by the seat of your pants and trying to keep up with the day traders. But if there's one thing you should take away from this book, it is this: there is another way. A way to make smart investments based on solid principles that reduce risk while creating the opportunity to outperform the market. And it's not some fly-by-night theory but a series of filters based on tried and tested financial strategic principles, backed by historical data, and purposefully selected to reveal opportunity based on real value. The 52-Week Low formula is not about finding cheap stocks that can be turned for a quick buck. It's a system, a process that takes the guesswork out of investing and removes the influence of human behaviors—fear, herding, peer pressure, and uncertainty—that can make investing difficult and disappointing.

Examining the five filters that represent the 52-Week Low formula individually reveals the building blocks for decision making that have formed the basis for not only my success but that of my clients, who, like you, were looking for a better, smarter way to invest their money.

Reviewing the Filters

Filter 1: Durable Competitive Advantage

Companies with a durable competitive advantage are companies that, by their nature and positioning, are difficult to compete with. Perhaps they are companies in unique industries for which the barrier of entry is too great to invite a lot of competition. A gravel-mining operation fits into this first camp. Getting into the gravel pit business is difficult, expensive, and time consuming. Those companies that already exist have insulated themselves from start-ups and newcomers because new businesses in an industry like that can't be profitable nearly fast enough to pose a threat.

There are "not in my backyard" (NIMBY) stocks—most municipalities will *not* vote for a new landfill—that have a great competitive advantage: waste management, gravel pits, companies people don't want in their neighborhoods but that are necessary to human function. These companies enjoy a moat built on societal morays.

And there are companies that make it hard for customers to leave. Banks offer direct deposit and Web bill pay to drive down the risk of their customers switching to a competitor. Most customers have zero interest in moving banks if they have their Web bill payments already setup with their existing banks. It can be painstaking to switch all of the existing bill payments to another bank. Because of these perceived switching costs, banks don't have to pay competitive rates, and payroll companies, like ADP and Paychex, can keep their profit margins high.

Car companies and airlines? Neither have NIMBY insulation or high switching costs. Great for the customer, terrible for the company's economics.

Perhaps they are companies with deep penetration to a broad variety of customers, making it impractical or, in some cases, impossible for new competitors to horn their way in. Visa and the industrial auction firm Ritchie Brothers are companies with clear and strong competitive moats.

Then there are the kinds of companies for which ultimately, consumers or regulatory powers have little to no influence over pricing. Often, companies or industries that seem like they have a durable competitive advantage actually don't. The steel industry comes to mind. There aren't many steel manufacturers left in the world—certainly not in the Western world. But government regulation of American steel manufacturing drives prices up, while those companies that purchase steel can get an identical product from a foreign producer for a lower cost. Ultimately, consumers and governmental oversight have way too much influence over the price of steel—driving it either up or down—for most producers to have a durable advantage.

Understanding a company's industry and positioning is crucial to understanding its value potential. That's why durable competitive advantage is so crucial to identifying whether they belong in the 52-Week Low formula.

Filter 2: Free Cash Flow Yield (Margin of Safety)

When identifying companies that fit into the 52-Week Low formula, it's important to look at not only the price of the stock but the value of the company from an owner's perspective. If you were to not just invest some money in the company but buy it, would it be worth it? Would taking on the whole company—assets and liabilities alike—yield a greater potential for value than simply putting your money into 10-year Treasury bonds?

Over the past 15 years working in this industry, I've come across dozens of clients and colleagues who've gotten themselves worked up by a particular stock. For example, look at Amazon, the e-commerce juggernaut that appears to have cornered the market on selling everything from books to dish soap. What do you think Amazon's free cash flow yield was as of January 24, 2014? Do you think buying a share of Amazon stock offered more free cash flow than a risk-free 10-year Treasury bond?

Believe it or not, on January 24, 2014, Amazon's free cash yield was .224 percent, while the 10-year Treasury bond was paying 2.75 percent in risk-free cash flow. The Treasury bond was paying 12 times the free cash flow you would earn from buying a share of Amazon.

It's one thing to get excited by a popular company and its global reach and want to put money into a company. It's another to look a little deeper and realize that, despite tremendous earnings and market share, the company as a whole generates less cash flow than the Treasury bond your grandmother bought you on your birthday.

Filter 3: Return on Invested Capital

Is the company earning more than its cost of capital (COC)? Why is this metric so important? The COC is what investors in the company demand on their investment, and if the company continues to deliver returns on invested capital (ROIC) less than the required rate of return (aka COC) of its investors, the investors will eventually go elsewhere and the company will disappear or dissolve or be bought by a competitor at a severe discount.

Good companies in good industries use their money to make more money. It's just that simple. They invest capital into projects—expansion, facilities, products—that will make them (and, by extension, you as the investor) more money.

There are white papers and books that discuss the importance of ROIC greater than COC and how this helps to identify companies with a durable competitive advantage. If a company doesn't possess a durable competitive advantage, over time its ROIC is equal to its COC because all the competition has driven down the excess ROIC.

Fiduciary management is crucial. A company's ability to spend money to make more money is a hallmark of good leadership and management and industry economics. And not just a little more money, but a lot more—whole new opportunities for revenue, and opportunities that, if handled well, will drive long-term value up. So, while it may be tempting to follow the latest craze, looking at a filter like ROIC reveals the likelihood that the company is creating incremental shareholder value.

Filter 4: Long-term Debt to Free Cash Flow Ratio

Can the company pay off its long-term debt in less time than it would take most people to pay off a car loan?

When we identify companies that have passed filters 1, 2, and 3, there is a high probability that the company will be able to generate positive free cash flow (FCF) for another three years. Any time beyond three years becomes too uncertain. I realize that many successful investors look at businesses that can pay off their long-term debts within five years or less, but to ensure that we have a sizable margin of safety we look at businesses that can pay off their long-term debts within three years or less.

It is hard for a company to go out of business if it has very little to no long-term debt. In fact, as we have seen in the past, when an economic recession occurs, it is often the unencumbered business that goes out on the hunt and buys its competitors or goes on the offensive as it relates to market share growth. We also discussed earlier in the book the downside protection that businesses with high-quality balance sheets provide to their shareholders during uncertain times.

Filter 5: The 52-Week Low

There's a good reason this is the fifth and final filter in the formula. Of the more than 2,800 companies on the New York Stock Exchange, perhaps 95 percent of them will be eliminated by the first four filters, leaving a greatly reduced list of well-positioned, well-managed companies that are prepared for the worst, invest their money wisely, and are structured to create lasting value to investors. How, then, do you choose which ones to invest in?

By looking at the ones with the greatest potential to provide the best return in the shortest time possible. Good companies, even great companies, go through slumps. A lot of factors can influence these dips; a lot can cause or exacerbate problems that leave a fundamentally strong company a little beat up. These are the companies this last filter is designed to identify, and it's a simple question that is asked: Is the company trading at or near its current 52-Week Low?

When most people talk about 52-week low stocks, they are talking about finding cheap stocks—penny stocks or something close to it. I'm not interested in finding the stocks that are the least expensive for me, or my clients, to buy. I'm interested in finding the ones that are the most likely to pay off in a short period of time with returns greater than I could achieve with a mutual fund or index fund in the same amount of time. I want companies that are poised and ready for a comeback. The 52-Week Low formula embodies the frontispiece found in the first edition of *Security Analysis*, written by Benjamin Graham and David Dodd in 1934.

In *Ars Poetica*, Horace said:

"Many shall be restored that now are fallen and many shall fall that now are in honor."

I can't stress this enough. The 52-Week Low formula is not about finding good prices but finding real opportunities for value. The real price of a company's stock is not nearly as important as its relative value—relative to historical performance, relative to its own standards. A good company may be trading at $1 or $350 a share. Both numbers are irrelevant. What is relevant is the relationship between that price and what it has been over the course of the previous year.

And among the companies that meet all of the requirements, 25 go into forming the 52-Week Low formula. Why 25? Quite simply, to hedge your bets. It's possible to use the filters in the 52-Week Low formula to identify a single stock, but remember what was written at the beginning of this chapter: no one can predict the future. Putting all your eggs into one stock basket is simply too risky. After all, even a great company may not be ready to deliver its potential value in six months' time. The CEO has a heart attack and dies, a shipping container leaks at sea, delays in the supply chain put off a product launch—there are a million things that can go wrong with a structurally sound company. Identifying a group of companies and investing in the group is a means of creating a bit of a safety net. All are primed and ready to create value, but all may not be ready at the same time. The 52-Week Low formula insulates from this problem by pitting a single company's shortfallings against 24 others with similar value potential, protecting your money and helping you sleep at night.

Your Part to Play

The 52-Week Low formula is a great tool to help enhance your chances of outperforming the market over time while participating less in down markets. It is an ongoing strategy that should help you make smarter decisions about how to invest your money, but the five filters above are certainly not the only parts of the equation. Perhaps the biggest variable in the plan is not an individual company's profit and loss, or even a group of companies' profits and losses, but the person reading this right now.

Success with the 52-Week Low formula requires a few things of you, as the investor:

- *Discipline.* To sell and review your investment every six months, regardless of gains or losses. The hardest thing to do in investing is to walk away from a winner or sell a company at a loss if it fails one of the filters. Most good companies make comebacks. The key is not to ride that comeback too long. You've got to walk away and identify new opportunities regularly in order to continue to find value in the formula.
- *Freedom from fears.* We all have biases. We all have fears. We are all capable of succumbing to our most basic desires to join a herd or keep up with the Joneses. Your best friend is making a killing on Apple? Ignore it. The talking heads on cable are raving about a new initial public offering? Change the channel. You've already got

a bunch of money tied up in a company that you just know will pull it all together with a new product? Divest and move on. Stop the bleeding and focus on having a process to identify value and the results should follow.

This is all extremely difficult to do, particularly in our modern age of 24-hour news and digital influence at our fingertips. Investing wisely is not about keeping up with the Joneses or the latest trends; it's about acknowledging fear and anxiety for what they are and having the courage to overcome them and trust in the principles.

- *Courage.* I can only assume that you're reading this because you're looking for a different way forward, that your instinct and research tell you that you could and should being doing better than you have been with your investments. First, I applaud your instincts. It was the exact same one I encountered 15 years ago—that nagging feeling that there was a better way. But stepping away from the known into the unknown is hard, no matter how right it feels in your gut. It took a lot of courage for me to begin thinking differently in an industry that rewards conformity so handsomely. But, looking back, that courage to follow my instinct and carve a new path forward has made all the difference in my life and in the lives of all those clients that have come along with me.

It will be hard at first, but I encourage you to give it a try. Have your investment manager contact me, or reach out yourself. That's what the 52-Week Low formula has been for me: an inspiration and a data-based foundation for a better path forward. I'm confident that it will be for you, too.

You just have to take the first step.

Afterword

Humans are horrible at predictions, and yet we allow fortune tellers to dictate the direction of our behavior. The world of investing is, perhaps, more susceptible to forecasting than others. Partly, this has to do with the emotional impact of our investment decisions. Will we have enough to retire? Can we get rich quick? Will we lose it all? It's hard to disassociate our emotions from our thinking, our instincts from our process. And, often, this difficulty in disassociation leads to disastrous consequences.

We tend to view people who are confident in their investment predictions with a certain amount of reverence. We assume they know more than we ever could. We put stock in that assumption and take risks based on a prediction that carries no guarantee of ever coming true. It's human nature, but the fact that something is in our nature does not mean it is inevitable.

As you've read through these pages, you might get the sense that I know what is going to happen next. I do not. Nor do any of the people I have long admired and often quoted in this book: James Montier, Howard Marks, Bruce Berkowitz, Benjamin Graham, Charlie Munger, and Warren Buffett. None of them know today what is going to happen tomorrow. But what these very successful people understand, what I understand, and what I hope you understand is this: There's no value in trying to predict what's going to happen tomorrow. The only real value is in preparing for whatever it might be.

The 52-Week Low formula is just that: a formula, a recipe, an approach. When you are cooking at home, you follow a recipe and expect certain results. You expect that the bread will rise, the meat with cook through, the vegetables will be perfect. You expect this because the recipe has been proven. But a proven recipe is not a promise of a good meal. Perhaps the thermostat on your oven is broken. Perhaps the flour was bad, the meat slightly frozen, the vegetables too old. Maybe the recipe was written for sea level and you're in the Rockies. Maybe the phone rings and you forget to stir. Any number of things can go wrong and ruin the meal. Does that make it a bad recipe? No. It just shows that recipes, like stock formulas and investment strategies, represent a path toward a desired outcome, not the outcome itself.

I didn't know the extent of the impact of the stock calamity of 2008 ahead of time. No one could have known what would actually happen during the dot-com burst. But just as Warren Buffett stayed away from tech in the late 1990s and I stayed away from bad real estate a decade later, so too do other smart investors typically avoid big failures by preparing for them. The 52-Week Low formula is meant to do that. There will be times when it will be wrong. Some of the businesses that end up on the list may not recover during the six-month period I buy them. But most of them seem to—at least they have, and I have no reason to believe they won't. Still, that's why I select 25 at a time—to prepare for the reality that not all of the undervalued companies that pass the filters realize gains.

That's the entire point here—to have a strategy that takes into account what can go wrong in order to take advantage of things going right. I am not a fortune teller. I have no crystal ball. And even if I did, I realize it would serve me better as a paperweight than as a strategy.

In the first chapter of this book, I quoted John Kenneth Galbraith, who said, "The only function of economic forecasting is to make astrology look respectable." It's a funny quote and true on a lot of levels. But the thing I want you to take away from it is this: seek not prediction when it comes to your investments, but, rather, prepare for the uncertain future by challenging conventional wisdom and pursuing a better path forward.

That's how you increase your chances of being successful in this game, by taking the long view and recognizing that not everything will go the way you hope it will go. Prepare for unexpected failure. Seek counsel from qualified people who aren't afraid to challenge your thinking.

Challenge my thinking.

Trust, but verify.

And, above all, *invert, always invert.*

About the Companion Website

This book includes a companion website, which can be found at **www.52weeklow.com**.

The website includes:

- Back-testing results of the strategy performed by Empiritrage.
- Back-testing results of the strategy performed by Morningstar.
- Monthly screen of stocks that might be eligible for purchase under the 52-Week Low screening process outlined in this book. This monthly service is merely for informational purposes only and should not be taken as an endorsement or recommendation of any particular company. The reader of this companion website should consult a registered investment adviser or registered dealer to receive personalized advice prior to making any investment decision. This service may be inconsistent or discontinue at any moment.

About the Author

Luke L. Wiley, CFP® CRPC®, is a Senior Vice President–Wealth Management at UBS Financial Services. He is a partner, with his brother, Zachary H. Wiley, CRPC® Vice President–Wealth Management, of Wiley Wealth Management at UBS Financial Services. Luke is the oldest of three brothers and grew up in a military family. He graduated from the University of Cincinnati with a triple major in Finance, Accounting, and Real Estate. He attended the University of Cincinnati on a soccer scholarship. In 2012, he ranked seventh out of 7,000 UBS financial advisors in terms of net new qualified relationships.

In more than 15 years in the Financial Services industry, Luke has been recognized as a thought leader and key strategist by clients, coworkers and industry leaders. He has been featured in several national publications for his team's approach to wealth management as well as his team's contrarian strategy to identifying and selecting stocks called the 52-Week Low Formula. In fact, in April 2013 he was featured in the "Advisor Profile" section in *Morningstar Advisor* magazine. Luke has been married to his lovely wife, Melissa, for over 16 years and together they have four healthy and loving children, Madyson, Jake, Leah, and Morgan, and live in Cincinnati, Ohio. He became financially independent by the age of 33 but shows no signs of resting on his laurels, as his motto is "I am a work-in-progress." He is committed to ongoing self-improvement, not only professionally, but also in his personal life.

   Luke is fascinated by human potential/achievement, behavioral psychology and finance, and the importance of proper decision-making. He believes one of the best guides to effective decision-making and the dangers of poor decision-making can be found in a book written around 3,000 years ago: the Book of Proverbs.

Author's Note

This publication is intended to provide helpful and informative material on the subject matter covered. It is sold with the understanding that neither the author nor the publisher is engaged in rendering professional services in the book.

Although great effort has been expended to ensure that only the most meaningful resources are referenced in these pages, the author does not endorse, guarantee, or warranty the accuracy, reliability, or thoroughness of any referenced information, products, or services. The existence of any particular reference is simply intended to imply potential interest to the reader.

The contents of this book should not be taken as personal financial or investment advice, or as an offer to buy or sell any securities, funds, type of fund, or financial instruments. It should not be taken as an endorsement or recommendation of any particular company, or individual, and no responsibility can be taken for inaccuracies, omissions, or errors. The reader should consult a registered investment adviser or registered dealer to receive personalized advice prior to making any investment decision.

The author does not assume any responsibility for actions or non-actions taken by people who have read this book, and no one shall be entitled to a claim for detrimental reliance based upon any information provided or expressed herein. The reader's use of any information provided herein does not constitute any type of contractual relationship between the reader and the provider(s) of this information. The author and publisher specifically disclaims any responsibility for any liability, loss, or risk, personal or otherwise, which is incurred as a consequence, directly or indirectly, of the use and application of any of the contents of this book.

Index